*Brookings Dialogues on Public Policy*

# The Future Role of the World Bank

ADDRESSES BY

*Robert S. McNamara, George P. Shultz,*
*Edward R. Fried, R. T. McNamar,*
*David Rockefeller, Manfred Lahnstein,*
*& A. W. Clausen*

EDITED BY

*Edward R. Fried & Henry D. Owen*

THE BROOKINGS INSTITUTION
*Washington, D.C.*

# The Future Role
# of the World Bank

# Brookings Dialogues on Public Policy

*The presentations and discussions at Brookings conferences and seminars often deserve wide circulation as contributions to public understanding of issues of national importance. The Brookings Dialogues on Public Policy series is intended to make such statements and commentary available to a broad and general audience, usually in summary form. The series supplements the Institution's research publications by reflecting the contrasting, often lively, and sometimes conflicting views of elected and appointed government officials, other leaders in public and private life, and scholars. In keeping with their origin and purpose, the Dialogues are not subjected to the formal review procedures established for the Institution's research publications. Brookings publishes them in the belief that they are worthy of public consideration but does not assume responsibility for their accuracy or objectivity. And, as in all Brookings publications, the judgments, conclusions, and recommendations presented in the Dialogues should not be ascribed to the trustees, officers, or other staff members of the Brookings Institution.*

# The Future Role of the World Bank

*Addresses by* ROBERT S. McNAMARA

GEORGE P. SHULTZ

EDWARD R. FRIED

R. T. McNAMAR

DAVID ROCKEFELLER

MANFRED LAHNSTEIN

A. W. CLAUSEN

*presented at a conference at the Brookings Institution*

*on January 7, 1982*

*Edited by* EDWARD R. FRIED

*and* HENRY D. OWEN

THE BROOKINGS INSTITUTION
*Washington, D.C.*

Library of Congress Catalog Card Number 82-71296
ISBN 0-8157-2929-4

9 8 7 6 5 4 3 2 1

# About Brookings

THE BROOKINGS INSTITUTION is a private nonprofit organization devoted to research, education, and publication in economics, government, foreign policy, and the social sciences generally. Its principal purpose is to bring knowledge to bear on the current and emerging public policy problems facing the American people. In its research, Brookings functions as an independent analyst and critic, committed to publishing its findings for the information of the public. In its conferences and other activities, it serves as a bridge between scholarship and public policy, bringing new knowledge to the attention of decisionmakers and affording scholars a better insight into policy issues. Its activities are carried out through three research programs (Economic Studies, Governmental Studies, Foreign Policy Studies), an Advanced Study Program, a Publications Program, and a Social Science Computation Center.

The Institution was incorporated in 1927 to merge the Institute for Government Research, founded in 1916 as the first private organization devoted to public policy issues at the national level; the Institute of Economics, established in 1922 to study economic problems; and the Robert Brookings Graduate School of Economics and Government, organized in 1924 as a pioneering experiment in training for public service. The consolidated institution was named in honor of Robert Somers Brookings (1850–1932), a St. Louis businessman whose leadership shaped the earlier organizaton.

Brookings is financed largely by endowment and by the support of philanthropic foundations, corporations, and private individuals. Its funds are devoted to carrying out its own research and educational activities. It also undertakes some unclassified government contract studies, reserving the right to publish its findings.

A Board of Trustees is responsible for general supervision of the Institution, approval of fields of investigation, and safeguarding the independence of the Institution's work. The President is the chief administrative officer, responsible for formulating and coordinating policies, recommending projects, approving publications, and selecting the staff.

v

# Contents

# Acknowledgments

CHARLS E. WALKER, former deputy secretary of the treasury and currently president of Charls E. Walker Associates, served as chairman of the conference. This report does something less than justice to his contribution, since it does not reflect his frequent interventions, marked throughout by humor and good sense, which kept the discussion lively and to the point.

We are grateful to Barbara Littell of the Brookings Advanced Study Program, who supervised the organizational arrangements efficiently and effectively, and to Nancy Davidson, who prepared the manuscript for publication.

The Brookings Institution is grateful to the Rockefeller Foundation for providing funds to help support the conference and the publication of this report.

*Edward R. Fried*
*Henry D. Owen*

*Washington, D.C.*
*April 1982*

ABOVE, LEFT:
*Henry H. Fowler*

ABOVE, RIGHT:
*George P. Shultz,*
*John W. Snyder*

RIGHT:
*Fred L. Hartley,*
*Robert S. McNamara,*
*Bruce K. MacLaury*

# Introductory Comments

EDWARD R. FRIED AND HENRY D. OWEN

SINCE THE WORLD BANK'S inception at Bretton Woods in 1944, its operations have been marked by growth and a high degree of adaptability. In its first decade, the Bank, then consisting solely of the International Bank for Reconstruction and Development (IBRD), concentrated on the reconstruction of Western Europe and Japan. After that, lending shifted to the developing countries, principally for infrastructure projects. The International Finance Corporation (IFC) was established as an affiliate in 1956 to encourage the expansion of the private sector. Another affiliate, the International Development Association (IDA), formed in 1960 to extend credit on soft terms, has provided a means of working with the poorest countries, which were not sufficiently credit-worthy to qualify for loans from the IBRD. In response to emerging problems in the 1970s, agriculture and then energy received high priority.

The World Bank Group is now the largest single source by far of publicly mobilized capital and technical assistance for development. It is also widely believed to be the most effective voice for economic efficiency and market-oriented policies in the developing world.

Despite this record, support for the Bank in the United States is now at its lowest point, and its future role is a matter of controversy. Similar doubts are not evident in other industrial countries, despite the fact that they supply three-fourths of the Bank's financial resources. Nonetheless, changing U.S. attitudes will be critical in shaping the Bank's future.

With this situation in mind, the Brookings Institution held a conference on January 7, 1982, to examine how the Bank might adapt to the changing environment of the 1980s. Participants included present and former U.S. officials; private bankers, industrialists, and academic experts; World Bank executive directors and management officers; and officials of other governments. All were familiar with the structure and operations of the Bank, and many understood from experience the difficulties of obtaining budgetary approval for the U.S. share of the resources needed to finance the Bank's present and future role.

The proceedings of the conference are reported in the body of this report. Included are the opening statement by Robert S. McNamara, former president of the Bank, on the outlook for developing countries; an address by R. T. MacNamar, deputy secretary of the treasury, outlining the administration's views on the role of the Bank and on desirable operating changes; and a closing statement by A. W. Clausen, president of the Bank, summarizing the impressions he had received during the day's discussions and giving his views on the future direction of Bank policies. The conference had panels on four subjects: the Bank and the private sector, energy investments, the relationship between multilateral and bilateral aid, and future financing of the Bank. Included in this report are the remarks by each panel's speaker and summaries of the other panelists' comments and subsequent general discussion.

No summary of the conference is provided; Mr. Clausen's closing remarks meet that need. Our purpose is rather to highlight four themes that emerged from the conference and pose policy issues for the United States.

First, it was generally agreed that the Bank should do much more to involve the private sector in development, such as:

—urging developing countries to join the General Agreement on Tariffs and Trade (GATT) and to accept the discipline of its rules, so that they can work to reverse protectionist trends and open world markets further;

—taking leadership in establishing a code for investment analogous to the GATT rules for trade;

—sponsoring a new mechanism to insure investments against political risks;

—providing more information and stronger incentives for private-sector cofinancing of Bank projects;

—expanding the IFC program.

This shift in emphasis is made necessary by a changing economic environment. Private sources (direct investment, commercial bank loans, and supplier credits) are now twice as large an element of net capital flows to developing countries as foreign aid, and have been growing faster. Further, the fact that manufactured exports provide the most rapidly expanding source of foreign exchange for the oil-importing developing countries indicates that they and the Bank should work harder to expand trade opportunities. Finally, the experience of the past two decades has demonstrated that countries giving the private sector wider scope have had the greatest economic success. In sum, the Bank can play a stronger role in enabling the developing countries to participate more productively in the international trade, payments, and investment system.

Second, speakers and commentators pointed out that emphasis on the private sector does not diminish the need for concessional assistance to the poorest countries through IDA. The infrastructure financed by IDA credits and the market-oriented policies that these credits enable the Bank to advocate are prerequisite to expanded private-sector activity in these countries.

This poses a difficult policy issue for the United States, which is the only country to fall behind in its contributions to the current IDA program and seems to be alone among the donor countries in seeking reductions in future replenishments of IDA. If the United States continues on this course, it will probably trigger reductions in the contributions of other countries and cause a sharp reduction in the IDA program. As a result, there will be fewer opportunities for the private sector to develop and slower progress toward economic improvement and ultimate self-reliance in the poorest countries.

Third, there was general agreement that the meeting would not have served its purpose if it left the impression that the only issue confronting the Bank was whether it needed more resources. In a changing economic and budgetary environment, the Bank's policies should be under constant scrutiny. Modifications presently worth exploring relate not only to the increased private-sector activity referred to earlier, but to new cofinancing techniques, flexibility in lending terms, acceleration of the graduation process, and reductions in the time required to prepare projects. Most of the discussants on energy assistance also suggested that new techniques as well as expanded energy lending are needed if the Bank is to fulfill its potential in helping developing countries reduce their dependence on oil imports. In general, resources will be scarce; new means should be devised to use them to maximum effect.

Fourth, concerns were expressed at the meeting about simultaneously reducing U.S. financial and political support for the Bank and inducing the changes in Bank policies described above. Doubts about U.S. support would weaken the Bank's credit standing on private markets and make it difficult for the Bank to borrow the amounts necessary to finance its lending program, thus reducing its ability to influence economic policies in borrowing countries. Bilateral U.S. aid has an important role, but it cannot mobilize the resources and economic influence that multilateral lending generates. Declining U.S. influence in the Bank, which would be a consequence of declining U.S. financial support, would also make it more difficult to persuade both lending and borrowing member countries to move toward the greater private-sector role and other changes in Bank policy that the United States favors.

Having outlined these general themes, which recurred in various forms throughout the discussion, we now make some brief concluding comments of our own.

The U.S. administration is surely right in urging the Bank to place increasing emphasis on, and to devise new means for, involving the private sector in development. This is where the potential for attracting additional capital and technology is greatest and the record most impressive. The Bank has many assets: a worldwide reputation for integrity and competence, a tradition of pragmatic economic analysis, a mandate in its charter to work with the private sector, and—above all—financial resources so large as to cause even the most statist of the developing countries to pay some heed to its counsel.

There is a tendency to go on from this position, however, to argue that by encouraging more private investment the Bank will need to provide fewer financial resources itself. We are convinced that this argument is wrong and that the reverse is more nearly correct. The evidence is strong that the Bank's financial and technical presence in a project has been a catalyst for private investment not only because of the counsel it offers and the infrastructure it helps to create, but also because it provides a form of political and commercial risk insurance for private participants. For the Bank to do more to attract private involvement in development will thus require the additional financial resources that are prerequisite to this continuing presence— including, as noted earlier, IDA credits for the poorest countries that cannot afford to service hard loans.

Financing for IDA, which looms as the most difficult budgetary issue ahead, could require a change in the traditional way this issue has been viewed. The conventional wisdom, as noted earlier, is that a cut in the U.S. IDA contribution would cause the other donor countries to follow suit, thus reducing the program by four times the U.S. shortfall. This would be understandable, but it is not a foreordained reaction. Other countries, led by Japan and Germany, could find a compelling case for maintaining IDA, in

President Clausen's words, as "a hardheaded investment in international trade, economic growth, and greater global stability and cohesion." On these grounds, they could decide to meet their commitments to the present IDA program on schedule and thereafter negotiate replenishments on the basis of their own priorities, recognizing that the United States might well do less, at least in the present period of budgetary stringency. Even if the U.S. share in financing IDA thus declined sharply for a while, the program could be held mostly on course.

These comments on resources for the Bank Group lead to the consideration of a key question that was put to the conference: who should have access to the pool of scarce world savings? Surely the criterion should be the efficiency that can be expected in the use of these resources. Bank projects typically have high economic rates of return, probably well above the world average. The Bank is needed as an intermediary to finance these projects, in part because market imperfections make it difficult for some countries to gain direct access to international capital. On the face of it, then, the Bank is an unusually effective allocator of resources, helping through its lending program to bring about an optimum use of world savings. And if the results of Bank lending are to promote greater private-sector activity, a likely additional contribution to world efficiency can be counted to its credit.

In short, the Bank advances the general interest in a more productive world. This is also the interest of the United States.

# Developing Countries and the World Bank in the 1980s

## ROBERT S. McNAMARA

I HAVE BEEN asked to talk about the outlook for the developing countries and the role of the World Bank in the 1980s. I accepted this invitation with considerable reluctance. Not only do I not wish to second-guess my successor, but I think it highly unlikely that during the past six months, when I have been away from the Bank, I have gained insights into the development problems and processes which I failed to achieve or express during the previous thirteen years or that I am now in a position to suggest changes in the World Bank for the 1980s which I did not put into effect in the 1970s. Despite my misgivings and to stimulate your discussion, I will try to address both topics.

*The outlook for the developing countries*

I believe that, during the first half of the 1980s and, as a matter of fact, for most countries throughout the decade, economic policymaking and investment programs will be dominated by the need to adjust to the very dramatic changes in the terms of trade these countries have experienced in the last two years. It is only to this aspect of the development problems which these countries will face in the 1980s that I wish to address myself before I turn to the role of the Bank.

As you all know, financial payments among nations are today in disequilibrium. Many of the oil-exporting nations are running very large current account surpluses. The oil-importing nations, as a group, including both the members of the OECD [Organization for Economic Cooperation and Development] and the developing countries, are running very large current account deficits.

The disequilibrium, or the economic imbalance, of course is not simply the existence of current account surpluses in some countries and deficits in others. That is a normal condition for countries at different stages of economic development. Rather, the disequilibrium reflects the fact that the deficits of the oil-importing developing countries are so high that they cannot be sustained indefinitely. Were they to be financed by external borrowings for more than a few years, the associated debt service would build up to such levels that it could not be supported by any foreseeable expansion of export earnings. Therefore, the current account deficits of the oil-importing developing countries will be reduced. The only question is whether the resulting equilibrium will be achieved at high or low rates of economic and social growth in the developing countries and with positive or negative effects on the economies of the industrialized world.

The deficits of the oil importers are, of course, the mirror images of the surpluses of the oil exporters. The surpluses, and hence the corresponding deficits, will disappear only when the oil exporters import more or export less. But there is a limit on how fast such capital surplus oil-exporting countries as Saudi Arabia, Kuwait, and the United Arab Emirates can expand their imports.

Therefore, if their oil exports are maintained at approximately present levels, and if oil prices in real terms remain approximately constant following the present glut, then the current account surpluses of the oil exporters will inevitably remain large for some years to come. And the oil-importing countries as a group must continue to incur the offsetting deficits for the same period of time.

Because the principal source of the growing imports into the capital surplus oil-exporting nations is the OECD nations, their current account deficits will be reduced faster than those of the oil-importing developing countries.

Throughout most of the 1980s the current account deficits that balance the current account surpluses will be incurred primarily by the oil-importing developing countries. There is no way by which they, as a group, can avoid the deficits other than a sharp reduction in their imports of oil or other goods. But such a reduction in imports would not only greatly reduce the rates of social and economic advance in those developing countries, it would also exert severe deflationary pressure on the economies of the countries from which they import, that is, the OECD nations.

If the world economy is to avoid these penalties, it is essential that the current account deficits of the oil-importing developing countries be financed at levels (averaging at least $70 billion to $80 billion per year for the next five to ten years) that will permit the maintenance of reasonable rates of economic and social advance, while their governments introduce the structural changes in their economies that will eventually make it possible for them to pay for the higher-priced oil through an exchange of goods.

These structural adjustments are going to be painful. In essence, they will require cutting back consumption from what would otherwise have been possible and reallocating the resources saved by this process to an expansion of exports or a substitution of imports.

Adjustment policies will have to cover a wide field, including increases in domestic food production, improved efficiency in resource use, a higher level of domestic savings, and, in particular, an expansion of domestic energy production.

If the adjustment process is to be carried out at high levels of growth, with consequent benefits to all nations, both developed and developing, it will require substantial assistance from both the capital surplus oil-exporting countries and from the members of OECD in order to assure adequate recycling of financial resources and maintain an open trading environment.

The danger of a rising tide of protectionism is great, but I am not going to talk about trade today. Instead, let me speak only of the problem of assuring adequate recycling of financial resources.

Recycling, after all, is not a problem in the aggregate sense because the surplus provides the means for its own financing. It becomes a problem, however, because the surplus does not get channneled automatically to countries in accordance with their balance of payments financing needs. Thus, adequate recycling mechanisms are necessary, both to channel private flows to deficit countries and to supplement them by public flows to the extent that the private flows fall short of the genuine balance of payments and the needs of the developing countries. It is in this perspective that we need to review the prospects for external flows to the oil-importing developing countries in the 1980s.

To me, it appears very unlikely that the commercial banks will be able to play the same role in the recycling of OPEC [Organization of Petroleum Exporting Countries] surpluses in the 1980s as they did during the 1973–79 period. During the 1970s, there was a remarkable increase in the role of the private markets in financing the large current account deficits of oil-importing developing countries which built up following the first set of oil price increases in 1973. (The deficits rose from $9 billion, or 2.4 percent of their gross national product, in 1970 to $39 billion, or 5.2 percent, in 1975.) As a result, by the end of 1980, total developing country debt had reached $440 billion (compared to about $68 billion in 1970), of which two-thirds was held by private lenders, compared to one-third in 1970.

As we all know, this remarkable increase in commercial bank lending was instrumental in producing economic growth in many middle-income developing countries as well as contributing to a high level of world economic activity. But it has also led to rising debt levels, an increase in interest costs, shorter debt profiles, and greater exposure of commercial banks in developing countries. These developments need to be watched carefully in projecting private flows in the 1980s.

It was for these reasons that last June the World Bank projected a substantially lower rate of growth in private market lending in 1980–90 (8 percent per year in nominal terms) compared to the 1970s (31 percent per year).

This analysis leads me to a point which I believe is central to devising adequate recycling mechanisms for the 1980s. Throughout much, if not all, of the decade, official flows from governments and multilateral institutions must supplement private flows to a far greater extent than during the 1970s if the legitimate needs of the developing countries are to be met. The international financial institutions, particularly the International Monetary Fund [IMF] and the World Bank, but regional banks as well, carry a heavy responsibility in this situation. These institutions were created to serve as intermediaries in the market and to play the role that the private market could not play. It would be ironic if their expansion were to be slowed down precisely at the time when the health of the entire world economy would be adversely affected by failure to assure smooth financing of the expanding deficits of the developing countries.

This is the essential perspective from which we must examine the adequacy of the recycling mechanisms for the 1980s. What we need is an overall framework in which the private flows would continue to expand but would be supplemented by rising levels of official flows. The multilateral institutions would play a balancing role and would provide the types of finance, technical assistance, and macroeconomic policy advice not available from other sources.

*The role of the World Bank*

This, then, brings me to the role of the World Bank in the 1980s. The Bank must assist, of course, in the recycling process. For this purpose its lending programs should be expanded beyond the levels planned before the recycling problem became apparent. But any such expansion would have to be carried out in the face of severe budgetary constraints in the OECD nations. Are these not contradictory objectives? I think not. Let me tell you why.

The most serious, although quantitatively smallest, requirement for additional external funds is in the poorest countries—those historically receiving only concessional assistance, including IDA credits. It is precisely these funds which are in shortest supply. However, the creditworthiness of some of IDA's borrowers has increased over the last decade. It should be possible, therefore, to replace a portion (but not by any means all) of their IDA (or comparable bilateral) borrowing with IBRD-type funds. By this means, resources would be released for the even poorer countries, which remain ineligible for private market borrowing or for IBRD-type financing. Furthermore, of the bilateral official development assistance, in 1980 only one-third was focused on the poorest countries: they actually received less assistance *per capita* than did the middle-income nations. Clearly, a reallocation of bilateral aid between the middle-income and the poorest countries is justified and needed.

Replacement of a portion of the IDA lending with IBRD lending and a transfer of bilateral aid from middle-income to low-income countries will, in itself, require an expansion of IBRD commitments. They need to be expanded for other reasons as well: the initiation of lending to China, the offset of higher than anticipated inflation rates, and, in particular, the expansion of lending for the financing of domestic energy production.

That increase in IBRD lending must, and I believe can, be financed with little or no call on the budgets of the industrialized nations. Has not the Bank reached the stage where, after thirty-five years of no defaults, with over $3 billion of reinvested earnings, a nearly one-to-one debt equity rate, and annual profits of several hundred millions of dollars a year, it can expand its borrowing capacity by increasing subscribed capital, without calling for payment of any of the subscriptions? In that case, the Bank's borrowing power, and hence its lending capacity, would be increased without the use of government funds.

A substantial expansion of IBRD lending, along with comparable support from the IMF and the regional banks, would help supplement private market assistance to the middle-income countries. But even after a reallocation of IDA and bilateral aid funds toward the poorest countries, it is likely that their social and economic advance will continue to be penalized by a shortage of external funds. To meet this need, I see no alternative to a substantial increase in the levels of IDA funds that are now authorized or planned.

Just the opposite is occurring. IDA, the largest single source of external funds to the poorest countries, is on the verge of being destroyed. As you know, the agreement for the sixth replenishment provided for commitments averaging $4 billion per year for fiscal years 1981, 1982, and 1983, of which the U.S. share was 27 percent, or $1,080 million. Against these sums, the Congress has appropriated $520 million in fiscal year 1981 and $700 million in fiscal year 1982—a reduction of 44 percent, and the other donors—including Britain, Germany, Japan—taking advantage of an escape clause in the agreement, propose to lower their contributions by the same amount.

I do not want to exaggerate, but I do believe that if these actions are not reversed, many of the poorest countries in the world, including some of the very large ones, are doomed to economic and political chaos in the decade ahead.

What should be done? Action is needed by the United States and by other industrial donor governments, independently of each other. The United States should support IDA lending (that is, "commitments") in the amount and on the time schedule originally agreed to ($4 billion per year for 1981, 1982, and 1983). I would hope that the appropriations required to support such lending could be attained by granting IDA a higher priority within the constrained federal budget.

The other OECD nations, almost all of whom face fiscal problems at least as great as ours, are, as a group, financing development assistance at levels in relation to income 65 percent greater than the United States. U.S. development assistance, as a percentage of GNP, has fallen 90 percent since the days of the Marshall Plan. During the same period our per capita income has doubled in real terms. The U.S. performance can only be described as disgraceful.

If this approach is not acceptable, however, then I repeat a statement I frequently made in the 1960s while serving as secretary of defense: at the margin—and here we are talking of only a few hundreds of millions of dollars per year—I believe the United States buys more security by spending a dollar for development assistance than for military hardware. Economic advance will not guarantee political stability, but long-continued economic stagnation will assuredly lead to political disorder.

As for the other donors to IDA, I see no justification whatever for reductions in their IDA sixth replenishment commitments or extensions of the period covered by those commitments. The needs of the poorest countries are greater today than they appeared to be at the time when the agreement was negotiated, and contributions to IDA have been fiscally budgeted and legislatively authorized and appropriated by the donor nations. They should instruct the Bank to proceed with the original IDA lending program.

So much for the Bank's contribution to the recycling process— it should be an essential part of its activities. But in the 1980s the Bank must be much more than a source of external financial assistance. To a far greater degree than in the 1970s, the Bank faces an opportunity for expanding its intellectual role—its consulting, advisory, and technical assistance activities.

Let me give you four examples.

1. Developing countries today need far more macroeconomic policy advice than they are receiving. The structural adjustment problems these countries will continue to face in an increasingly complex economic environment—an environment of low rates of growth in their export markets, highly volatile commodity prices, rapidly fluctuating interest rates, floating exchange rates, rising debt levels—will accentuate their need for this assistance. There has been a major shift during the past ten years in the willingness of the developing countries to seek and accept the Bank's advice in economic policy. I can think of no service which the Bank could offer with "higher leverage."

2. The Bank's (and the world's) research in the fields of international economics and development is grossly inadequate in relation to the magnitude of the problem. Were the Bank, in addition to what it finances through projects, to devote as little as 10 or 15 percent of its annual income, say roughly $50 million per year, to such research, including the development of research institutions in the developing countries, it could make an immense impact in the world's understanding of the development process. The research that addressed both the macro and the micro problems of economic development would be very important, including such matters as the effect of protectionism on individual countries, changes in trade patterns, small-scale industrial development, rigidities in the recycling process, the problem of the landless poor (26 percent of the labor force in many developing countries), and the cause and cure of very low or even negative growth rates in many of the low-income countries, particularly those of sub-Saharan Africa. The size and importance of such a research effort can be gauged by noting that the total annual expenditures of the Brookings Institution, the American Enterprise Institute, Resources for the Future, and the new Institute for International Economics probably do not exceed $35 million.

3. Many developing countries are now asking for technical assistance to develop their private sector. During the latter part of the 1970s, an increasing number of the countries in Asia, Africa, and Latin America have indicated that they wish to strengthen and expand their private sectors. They need advice on the legal structure required, appropriate incentives for stimulating savings and investment, and the organization of financial markets. The Bank has barely begun to provide such services on the scale required. There is an immense opportunity to strengthen the private sectors in the developing countries. But having said that, I also wish to emphasize that no likely expansion of that sector and of the external equity investment in it will substitute for the public investment, both domestic and foreign, required to finance the necessary infrastructure and the expansion of agriculture and social services required for reasonable levels of social and economic advance.

4. Many of the so-called high-income countries approaching or exceeding what in the past has been considered the Bank's "graduation guideline" will continue to need technical assistance from the Bank. We should recognize that more than ever before countries such as Yugoslavia that may be nearing traditional "graduation" trigger points do need macroeconomic advice as well as continued financial assistance as they face highly volatile private capital markets and disruptive trade conditions.

To meet demands such as these would mean that the Bank would be forced to expand its staff per dollar loaned. Its program of operations during the 1980s would then become far more labor-intensive.

Let me conclude my remarks by repeating what I said earlier. In my opinion, during the 1980s the economies of the oil-importing developing countries will be dominated by a global adjustment process. The Bank can play a major role—contributing both financially and intellectually—in facilitating that process. The result would be economic, political, and security benefits to the United States. As a nation, will we be wise enough to provide the Bank the political and financial support it needs to fulfill that role? We are not doing so now. I hope we will in the future.

# The World Bank and the Private Sector

## GEORGE P. SHULTZ

IN THIS WORLD of risk and turmoil, the Bank must adapt its policies and activities to the problems as they are and as they are evolving. Certain observations about the process of development, taken in the light of the Bank's charter, lead to a conclusion that the Bank must give more emphasis in its projects to its relations with private capital and private entrepreneurship. As the Bank develops this emphasis, consideration should be given to work in the areas of trade, investment, and national economic policies, and to use of concessional aid—scarce under the best of circumstances—in a manner that yields the greatest leverage and emphasizes the comparative advantage of the concessional lending function.

*The problems of risk, uncertainty, and turmoil for economic development*

Uncertainty is a constant in business and financial circles, heightened as it is by high interest rates, country-content requirements, predatory interest-rate subsidies, expropriation by whatever name, and the fluctuations of the dollar. Slow growth on a world scale, interruptions or threatened interruptions of essential supplies, rapidly changing comparative advantages that challenge established and large-scale industries in developed countries—all these and more are influences that tend to turn countries inward. The pressures are intense to protect what is at home on the one hand and, on the other, to race for markets abroad through exports protected by government-backed subsidies, guarantees, and non-market pressures. There is even a suggestive irony to the very success of the rounds of tariff reduction, as we now see emerging in their place more arbitrary and unpredictable forms of protection. Now that the taboo seems to have been placed on tariffs, determined interest groups seek to protect themselves in subtle and less visible ways.

These escalated levels of uncertainty take their toll. The volume of world trade, after decades of sustained growth, has been falling in real terms over the past year. Major investment decisions are postponed or demand an extraordinary rate of return to justify the assumption of risks imposed by the prospect of sudden and unpredictable action by government. Economic development, for which political stability is a necessary if not sufficient condition, is cruelly disappointing in many countries.

As in many contests, the best defense can be a good offense. I say that in the realm of economic policy we should go on the offensive again. We should be capable of raising our aspirations by thinking on a grand scale and of maintaining momentum through careful and realistic work on particular and difficult issues. Fortunately, in the economic sphere, we have one great fact going for us: all can gain together from healthy economic development, investment, and trade. In the parlance of the day, ours is a positive, not a zero-sum, game.

Our offensive should focus on long-term commitments, since it takes time for confidence to build and for policies to bear their fruit. The offensive must address the rules for trade as expressed in the GATT, the conditions for foreign investment, the stimulation of economic development in less developed countries, and attention to the international consequences of national economic policy, especially that of the United States. Can the trading nations of the non-Communist world reach a greater measure of agreement and understanding in such a wide range of related areas? If they can, they reduce the level of uncertainty in the operation of the world economy. The assurance and cohesion attained would in turn constitute the basis for increased trade and investment and for economic advance in developing and developed countries alike.

**The development process**

The Bank's charter (as summarized in the 1981 annual report) sets out some sensible rules to govern its operations:

1. Lend only for productive purposes.

2. Stimulate economic growth in the country to which loans are made.

3. Pay due regard to prospects for repayment.

4. Loan to governments or with government guarantees (a way of assuring the approval of the government of the country involved).

5. Make decisions to lend based only on economic considerations.

The development process leads to emphasis on each country's own economic policies. *Domestic* savings and *domestic* investment play a key role. Valid price signals are essential, whatever the level of development. The market approach has succeeded, and the command approach has failed.

Taiwan, Singapore, and Hong Kong show what the Chinese can do in a market environment. The real GNP per capita on Taiwan is about four times that in the People's Republic of China. Chile during and after communism provides a dramatic contrast: at the end of Allende's regime, there was economic chaos, with inflation running at more than 600 percent; since 1975, there has been sustained real growth of over 7 percent per year, with inflation now under control—down to about 12 percent. The incompetence of agriculture in the Soviet Union is demonstrated every year. The standard of living in East Germany suggests that Germans can do well under almost any circumstances, but real GNP per capita in the West is almost twice that in the East.

When the Bank lends on the basis of economic considerations only, as required by its charter, this evidence of which kind of economies have been successful and which have not should be taken into account.

Four avenues to prosperity link North and South: international trade; investment from outside, drawing on savings in other countries; technology transfer—a valid preoccupation these days and one that imposes responsibilities on host, as well as guest; and concessional aid, which draws on world savings, applied to areas of comparative advantage and also used as a lubricant to private financial flows.

*Creation, not transfer, of wealth*

The creation of wealth, not its transfer, is what counts in development: it is possible; it is sustainable; and it assumes a complementary rather than an adversary relationship between North and South. We need to adjust our rhetoric accordingly. The old rhetoric—emphasizing the transfer of wealth—is counterproductive because it reflects an incorrect view of what leads to development. It can deceive poor countries into not doing for themselves, because they are led to believe that there is an easy way. Also, it increasingly alienates the developed countries.

*The Bank's legitimate interest in trade*

The protectionist tide must be of special concern to developing countries. They need markets for their goods and services. That is why they should be signatories to GATT, with all the standing that membership gives to raise the alarm when others violate or evade the rules, and with the discipline for their own long-run development objectives imposed by those very rules.

The task involves the extension of the GATT framework so that less developed, as well as industrialized, countries are included more fully in its coverage. The Tokyo Round agreement carries the signatures of 25 countries, whereas 141 countries are members of the World Bank. The exports of nonsignatory countries constitute about 35 percent of total world exports and are gaining in proportionate terms. That 35 percent in 1980 amounted to some $650 billion in value. Obviously, the special needs and problems of less developed countries must be recognized if this effort for greater coverage is to succeed. The prospect of mutual advantage is a legitimate and potentially strong propellant if it can be linked to the right political atmosphere.

*An agreement for investment*

If the investment needed for economic development is to be forthcoming, the conditions for that investment must be made more clear, more predictable, and more reliable. Investment is by its nature an undertaking for the long term. The investor properly bears or deals with commercial and technical risks of a wide variety; but if the return needed to justify action can be spared a large premium attributable to political uncertainty, the pace of investment will pick up sharply.

I therefore urge that our governments work out a code, a common base of understanding and agreed-upon rules for behavior, a sort of GATT for investment. The World Bank is ideally suited to undertake such a general agreement on investment. The Bank has:

—worldwide respect for its integrity and professional ability;

—a membership of 141 nations, spanning all stages of development, a point of special significance since agreement is needed across the board;

—a tradition of orientation to projects and pragmatic economic analysis;

—an announced readiness to work in conjunction with private capital, building on its long-term efforts in the IFC;

—an announced desire to stimulate greater flow of private capital to developing countries as a key to their economic development.

I am pleased to note that Tom Clausen, in his first address as president at the Bank's 1981 annual meeting, endorsed this idea and devoted a considerable portion of his address to its development. Obviously, his proposals for a multilateral insurance agency are also most responsive to this point.

If this important task is undertaken, those involved will have a wealth of experience and effort from which to draw. I call attention to a few items as illustrations: the investment provisions of the Treaty of Rome; work by the OECD on international investments; the World Bank's efforts to encourage arbitration of investment disputes; and privately negotiated efforts to treat in creative ways the classic issues of ownership, control, responsibilities, and distribution of revenues.

The very fact that a general code for investment does not exist suggests that difficult issues are involved—for developed, as well as less developed, countries. The question is whether the difficulties are outweighed by the need—the need for investment and for the assurance and stimulation that a code could bring to the investment process.

*Technology transfer*

A code for foreign investment would be especially beneficial to developing countries. Private capital brings skills and technology along with resources. If political risk can be kept under control, then more projects can be justified and the payment periods envisaged for them can be more consistent with the long-term interests of investor and country alike. The more private capital is drawn into worthwhile projects, the more aid capital can be devoted to those aspects of development that do not lend themselves to a market approach.

I have had the opportunity and privilege of taking part in this investment process, with the projects involved covering a wide range of industries in many countries. I see a great variety of ways in which ownership, control, responsibility, and flow of funds can be arranged to suit varying aspirations and abilities. Projects can be engineered and constructed in a manner that builds national skills and professional abilities, transferring essential human technology in the process.

My own company, for example, has conducted its project work in ways that have raised the levels of skill, professional competence, and managerial abilities of over 100,000 people throughout the developing world during the last five years alone. When we build a project in a developing country, we try to do it in a way that leaves behind not just a plant that will work, but people who know something about how to make it work and how to build another one, and who have skills they did not have before. I may add more than parenthetically that our own people also learn and develop in this same process. In these and many other ways, the process of foreign investment and foreign involvement in the development process can serve objectives beyond those involved in each investment taken by itself.

*Concessional aid*

Aid starts with an open and unselfish attitude. Aid continues with the recognition that trade with and investment in developing countries is clearly of great benefit to those developed countries that provide aid. Aid money involves subsidies that can vary widely in degree and form to suit country circumstances and stages of development. Beyond substantive merit, aid can and does give fabric to a world sense of society, where people do care about each other and about the ideas of fairness and opportunity.

Remember that savings are a scarce resource. Aid should be used as a supplement to, not a substitute for, private capital. This means the use of aid in areas of comparative advantage, such as education, health, and building infrastructure. But local partners, probably the government, should be sought for these types of projects.

Operational points deserve renewed attention. For example, time in developing World Bank projects is long—two to three or even more years. Such delays can increase total project and related opportunity costs through inflation, delay of project income, and so on, by 50 percent or more. These cost increases then must be financed. Simply by increasing the turnaround time and efficiency of its approval processes, the World Bank could directly assist in reducing project costs, thereby increasing project viability and decreasing the need for funding these costs of delay. This in turn would help the World Bank spread its resources further.

Cofinancing should get increasing emphasis, as Tom Clausen has clearly said. It can be an important adjunct to reduction of political risk; it leverages the money that concessional aid can bring; it involves people from the private investment world, who bring technology and expertise; and it gives another test, a kind of market test, beyond the Bank's own analysis to a given project.

*The Bank in a new and changing environment*

The World Bank is not just a special lending organization. The true purpose of the Bank is economic development and, noting its formal title, not just in less developed countries. As a leading custodian of this central idea, it must take an interest in all the factors affecting development.

Deterioration in the openness of the trading system poses a tremendous threat to all economies, perhaps especially those struggling from a low base of development. The coming GATT ministerial meeting and the preparations for it can be of vital significance to the rules for trade. The World Bank should be a part of this process.

Political and military risks create premiums for investment that reduce its flow and contribution. The World Bank should lead in the process of creating a GATT for investment and in parallel insurance efforts.

Domestic economic policies, domestic savings, and domestic investment are the keys to development. This point needs to be kept in the forefront, not as a matter of ideology, but as a practical and operational application of the "economics only" test drawn from the Bank's charter.

Concessional aid can play a critical role in economic development. As an allocation from the limited flow of overall world saving, aid is a scarce and precious resource. Use it with a boldness that cares and is careful. Associate it with the constructive instincts and abilities of others. Parlay it into a place at the table wherever the rules for trade and investment are worked out.

The process of economic development is threatened by unsettled and uncertain conditions. In the sphere of economics, this is the time for a fresh offensive on behalf of hard but constructive actions. We all know how easy it is to be critical, but we also know how worthwhile it is to be constructive.

## Summary of Comments by John M. Hennessy

IN REVIEWING the Bank's relations with the private sector, the following four propositions should be taken into account. As a group, they point to a different, but even more important, role for the Bank in the future.

1. New institutional arrangements are needed in the area of trade and investment, as George Shultz has emphasized. The Bank could help to bring these arrangements into being if it chose to assert itself. It could become a policeman for GATT in respect to trade relations between industrial and developing countries and could perform a similar function in the investment field.

2. The Bank should act more as a catalyst to promote and mobilize private capital than as a direct lender. This role will require a different philosophy of project selection and different performance standards to replace emphasis on the number and value of annual loans.

3. Much more should be done to promote the private sector through Bank loans for infrastructure, joint venture projects, local development banks, and privately owned agriculture.

4. Most of the suggestions for leveraging the Bank's resources through such changes as increasing the gearing ratio, reducing liquidity ratios, or eliminating paid-in capital are probably unwise. They would not be helpful from a financial point of view, and

trying to bring them about would distract the Bank from accomplishing needed changes in its role.

Specific suggestions, based on these propositions, include the following:

1. Provide political risk insurance through a separate affiliate, or in some other way.

2. Consider spinning off the IFC from the World Bank so as to give the former financial independence and a greater incentive to be self-supporting. The IFC could continue to participate in joint venture projects with the Bank but would raise funds from capital markets on its own. It could also establish a trust fund or subsidiary in which the other stockholders would be private institutional lenders in the industrial countries, whose capital at present is barely being tapped for development lending.

3. Steps to increase cofinancing could include: automatic cross-default clauses in cofinancing; completion guarantees on large-scale export or industrial projects; financing of back-end maturities with the Bank providing take-out financing for commercial paper or commercial bank loans; working-capital deficiency agreements on projects with volatile cash flows to achieve partial resource financing; production-payment agreements to finance reserves of energy and minerals with subsequent sell-down to the private sector; granting exchange-availability guarantees to countries engaged in structural adjustment or for long lead-time projects; and offering full guarantee for loans or capital market transactions for a project or entity that should eventually become eligible to borrow on its own credit.

4. The Bank, along with the Fund, should develop a standardized debt-reporting system for all countries receiving loans. The primary purpose of this information is to provide all banks with data that will allow them to satisfy the information requirements of their directors and regulators. It is almost incomprehensible that in 1982 this essential tool of domestic economic management does not exist in most developing countries. Lenders are wary of increasing exposure to nations where this kind of information is not available.

5. The private sector needs to have a better understanding of what the Bank does, particularly if its operations change as suggested above. There are many areas where the Bank can fill the information gap. Broad dissemination of project information is one; seismic data for drilling is another. Serious thought should be given to setting up a separate marketing department to accelerate the transfer of information.

## Summary of Comments by Henry D. Owen

THE BANK has had a remarkable record of success in contributing to the growth of the private sector in developing countries by using its influence to persuade these countries to follow market-oriented policies and to remove regulations that unnecessarily restrict private enterprise. The Bank's tenacity in insisting on effective economic policies in connection with its loans is attested to by the criticism it receives—both from government officials in industrial countries who would like to see loans made for short-term foreign policy reasons and from spokesmen for the Group of 77 and others who prefer an institution less dominated by a market philosophy and more willing to write blank checks to borrowing governments.

The Bank has been effective in stimulating private capital flows to developing countries, which increased from $9 billion in 1970 to $43 billion in 1979. The countries that the Bank has been most successful in bringing to an advanced state now receive most of their external resources from the private sector.

Evidence does not suggest that the Bank preempts private lending or investment; the record points in the opposite direction. By insisting on sound domestic economic policies, by giving its stamp of approval to a project or a sector, and by supplying funds, the Bank provides new opportunities for private foreign lending and investment.

A growing Bank role in the future, including concessional assistance for the poorest countries, will continue to be linked to rising private investment. For the poorest countries, infrastructure investments, which frequently are financed by IDA credits, are essential to build up the domestic private sector and to attract foreign investment and lending.

Further action is needed in two areas: increasing the information available to the private sector regarding cofinancing and IFC opportunities, and making cofinancing more profitable for private lenders. Hennessy's suggestions are very helpful in this connection.


## General Discussion

BURKE KNAPP, former World Bank senior vice-president, said that the difference between McNamara's call for an expanded World Bank role in recycling and Shultz's argument that Bank financing should not encourage countries to postpone necessary adjustments was more apparent than real. The fundamental point has been left out. The Bank does not provide balance of payments financing but lends for productive investments. Thus it serves as an intermediary institution that mobilizes savings and channels them to uses where economic returns are high. These loans facilitate structural adjustment; they in no way postpone it.

Former Secretary of the Treasury Henry Fowler pointed out that there had been agreement in the discussion that the Bank increases opportunities for the private sector and for the exports, lending, and investments of multinational companies. There was also no dissent from McNamara's concern that the political and legislative environment in the United States for some time now was undercutting U.S. leadership in the Bank and limiting the Bank's potential. As he saw it, the missing ingredient was an active role on the part of the U.S. private sector, in its own self-interest to say nothing of the national interest, to gain support for the Bank in the Congress and in the administration. Something more was necessary than the annual round-robin letter to Congress sent by ex-secretaries of the treasury in support of appropriations for the Bank.

Owen suggested that the private sector, including industry, church groups, and others, was effective in supporting the Bank, but that the executive branch needs to do a better job in alerting these groups when the need for support arises.

Shultz said that support for the Bank had eroded; going down the same road and recommending more of the same would not meet the problem. Private-sector involvement in development has three strands—trade, investment, and finance. In each the Bank should be searching for an expanded role to meet requirements in the 1980s. In trade, the Bank should be pressing the developing countries to join in the drive for a more open trading system by themselves accepting obligations in the General Agreement on Tariffs and Trade. In investment, could the Bank help to bring about a code for investment and a multinational program for insuring against political risks? The Bank should, moreover, be working harder in developing countries to put the private sector to work. Finally, Shultz said we should think of the problem in terms of access to a world savings pool; how much of these scarce resources should go to aid and how can this portion best be used? As a strong supporter of the Bank, he stressed that new initiatives were necessary to turn the situation around.

Hennessy endorsed these views.

Brookings President Bruce MacLaury said that while he understood how the Bank could adopt an advocacy role in the areas outlined by Shultz, its charter requires that lending decisions be made on economic criteria alone. Was Shultz suggesting that in considering a project for financing the Bank should insist that the country follow a private-sector philosophy as a condition for a Bank loan?

Shultz said he would not establish such a condition. He thought the need he had in mind could be met by drawing attention both to the success of those countries that had emphasized the private-sector route and to the fact that the surrounding environment has an effect on the chances of success of a particular project.

Former Secretary of the Treasury Joseph Barr asked what had happened to the proposal for lodging a center for the resolution of investment disputes in the World Bank.

Moeen Qureshi, World Bank senior vice-president, replied that the Center has been established and is operating, but that its functions are limited by the fact that both parties to a dispute must voluntarily accept its jurisdiction, which is rarely the case. Moreover, a number of developing countries, notably those in Latin America, are not members.

Jaime Garcia-Parra, World Bank executive director for a number of Latin American countries, said that the Bank was likely to play a greater role in promoting private capital investments as mining and energy assumed increasing importance in the Bank's portfolio. The Bank can play this role by helping to finance domestic counterparts in joint ventures with international companies and by providing technical assistance.

Ismail Khelil, Bank executive director for a number of North African and Southwest Asian countries, endorsed Shultz's suggestion for a comprehensive approach to development. This should include taking account of external factors that place a country's economic program in jeopardy, such as changes in the terms of trade. He also suggested greater effort to involve the capital surplus oil-exporting countries and give them more say in the operations of the Bank, reflecting any revision in their role in the Bank's capital structure.

Marc Leland, assistant secretary of the treasury for international affairs, asked for more suggestions about possible changes in the Bank that would adapt it more effectively to a changing world and help to meet congressional concerns. He said that real increases in resources were not likely; how then should existing scarce funds be allocated over the future? What countries should be cut; what about China? Should countries, even poor countries, that have but do not use access to capital markets continue to have access to the Bank? Can the Bank set effective conditions for its lending? In short, operating under the constraint of fixed resources will require difficult changes from the past, when resources available to the Bank increased steadily.

Charles Robinson, chairman of the Energy Transition Corporation, supported the notion that the Bank should play a larger role in trade and political risk insurance, and suggested that a new instrument was needed, such as an international resources bank, which was under consideration in the mid-1970s. He thought it would be useful to establish a task force consisting of representatives of the private sector, the Bank, and the developing countries to focus on these issues.

Said El Naggar, Bank executive director for a number of North African and Persian Gulf countries, stressed the complementary nature of the Bank's activities and those of the private sector. The effectiveness of the Bank in promoting the private sector is dependent on its presence in a country, and that in turn is reflected in the volume of its lending. In the poorest countries, a wider role for the private sector depends on creating infrastructure and credit and marketing institutions. Here too, the Bank's role, particularly IDA credits, can be crucial.

Marine Midland Bank president John Petty endorsed proposals to focus more attention on the Bank's trade role and on the problem of allocating its scarce resources. He stressed the need for private development banks in developing countries, where it is possible to get host country guarantees. He also thought that to encourage additional cofinancing the Bank may have to consider subordinating its own position as a lender, unpleasant as that prospect might be. In his view, commercial banks will continue to be active in recycling, but proportionately less than in the past.

N. Ram, correspondent for the *Hindu,* suggested that evidence did not bear out the contention that emphasis on the private sector always produced the right answer to the developing countries' economic and social problems. India's experience was an example. Moreover, how did this aspect of the discussion apply to China?

Fowler stressed that he was not endorsing the status quo; he did insist that the Bank is more likely to evolve along the lines the U.S. private sector wants if that sector and the U.S. government actively support the Bank.

# The World Bank
# and Energy Investments

EDWARD R. FRIED

IN DISCUSSING the Bank's role in energy, we should bear two propositions in mind. The first is that energy is now a key determinant of the economic prospects of the oil-importing developing countries, and probably will continue to be through the end of this century. The second is that the ability of these countries to cope with their energy problems will exercise an important influence on the international economic system, specifically on world oil supplies, prices, and security, and on the health of international trade and finance.

These are substantial propositions, directly affecting industrial as well as developing countries. Yet much of the discussion and caution about expanding the Bank's energy program has revolved around two concerns, neither of which seems to be applicable.

The first concern is that the Bank's program in oil and gas could displace private investment. If that were so, of course, the Bank would be making no net contribution to solving the problem and there would be no justification for continuing, let alone expanding, its role in energy. In fact, a specified purpose of the Bank's oil and gas lending is to facilitate and expand private investment, not to replace it. In view of the Bank's track record and the guidelines for its oil and gas program, there is every reason to believe it will accomplish this objective. Incidentally, it is also well to remember that oil and gas lending, which is comparatively new for the Bank, represents about one-third of the Bank's energy program. The other two-thirds is in electric power and other energy sectors where the Bank has been lending for a long time and where requirements have accelerated, but fears about preempting private direct investment are not ever relevant.

The second major concern is budgetary cost. This would also be a serious matter, particularly in these times of budgetary stringency, if it were applicable. In fact, it should be possible to give the Bank wider opportunities to lend in the energy field at little or no immediate cost to the budgets of industrial countries

I propose to outline the energy problems of the oil-importing developing countries through a series of briefly documented assertions. Then I will discuss how the Bank could help.

*The problems*   High oil import costs have now become the biggest single constraint on the economic prospects of the oil-importing developing countries. It is evident that the rise in the oil import burden has led directly and indirectly to the dangerous increase in current account deficits and to the deterioration in debt-servicing capacity of these countries.

The energy constraint on growth in these countries will become worse unless remedial action is taken. Increasing use of energy is an essential part of the development process. Twenty years ago the developing countries used about 10 percent of the free world's commercial energy; today that proportion is 15 percent; and twenty years from now it is likely to be 25 percent. It is certainly possible for these countries to use energy more efficiently, but because of their low level of energy use and the steady substitution of commercial energy for traditional fuels they have less room for conservation as prices rise than has proven to be true in the industrial countries. If the oil-importing developing countries are to achieve above-average economic growth, which may well be a necessary condition for a reasonably satisfactory international order, they will have to have access to, and be able to pay for, an increasing proportion of the world's commercial energy.

The problem therefore can be stated as follows: while reversing the trend toward increased dependence on oil imports, the oil-importing developing countries will still need a steadily increasing volume of energy fuels to sustain economic growth. How can this be done?

One way is through increasing domestic production of energy fuels and increasing efficiency in the use of energy, which ultimately would save on oil imports.

A second way would be to expand exports more rapidly, particularly to the industrial countries, thus earning the foreign exchange to pay for oil imports. Export expansion in these countries has been rapid; in today's circumstances, however, continuing, let alone expanding, this pace would place inordinate pressure on the international trading system—more than its political foundations are likely to support.

A third way is through increased financing. This was a major aspect of adjustment to the first oil shock. As Bob McNamara pointed out, however, with outstanding debt already at a high level, continuing sizable increases in net borrowing are not likely to be sustainable.

Finally, these countries could be forced to balance their energy accounts through substantially reduced economic growth, which would be the most costly outcome for them and for the rest of the world.

After the first oil shock, trade and financing were the principal forms of adjustment. In the wake of the second oil shock, increasing energy production and increased efficiency in the use of energy will necessarily have to be more important, indeed a major form of adjustment.

A successful energy program in the oil-importing developing countries would also improve the economic outlook for the industrial countries. This clearly applies to the world oil market. The oil-importing developing countries are likely to be the principal source of increased demand on the world oil market for the indefinite future. To the degree that their oil import requirements are contained, oil will be in more ample and secure supply for all countries. The international trade and payments system would also benefit. A stronger adjustment effort in energy would ease balance of payments difficulties, improve debt-servicing capacity, and avoid strains on international capital markets.

Such an approach would require a massive increase in energy investment in these countries. Bank studies suggest that energy investments need to more than double over the course of this decade to a level of $40 billion to $50 billion a year (in 1980 dollars). This would represent about 3 percent of their GNP and 10 percent of total investment.

*The Bank's role*  All available sources of capital would need to be tapped: private and public, foreign and domestic. High oil prices in themselves will be the major force for shifting internal investment priorities to energy and for attracting foreign debt and equity capital, as they have been in the industrial countries. However, there are serious political, technical, and financial obstacles to the mobilization and efficient use of capital. This is where the Bank should come in, performing its traditional role of providing technical assistance, helping to formulate least-cost approaches, participating in financing, and through all this, encouraging the inflow of foreign debt and equity capital.

The Bank now plans to lend $14 billion (current dollars) for energy projects during the five years from 1982 to 1986, which would compromise about one-fifth of its lending program. This is the maximum it can now lend for energy without seriously compromising other high-priority programs, notably agriculture. If it had additional lending authority, the Bank believes it could easily double its energy program, all for projects with economic rates of return that are higher than the average opportunity cost of capital in the countries concerned or in the free world as a whole.

Even if its program were doubled—and this deserves emphasis—Bank lending would represent less than 10 percent of estimated investment requirements. The measure of the program's success is the extent to which, through its projects, advice, and technical assistance, it can attract additional domestic capital for energy and additional foreign capital and know-how to supplement domestic resources. In general, capital from other sources associated in Bank projects is about two to three times the amount of Bank financing.

The Bank's role in an expanded energy program would vary with the type of investment. Power development would be half the program. This has been a traditional sector of Bank lending. Higher oil prices have made it feasible to tap new hydroelectric sources, emphasize coal-fired thermal plants, and exploit geothermal sites. The Bank's contribution is to help in long-term planning, project preparation, and developing investment packages where its own funds can be associated with much larger amounts of debt capital and supplier credits.

Oil and gas would be about one-third of the program. This is a comparatively new program; project lead times are long; and the shape of the program is only beginning to evolve. Its purpose is to expand total investment, which necessarily means helping to create conditions that would attract additional participation by the international industry. It is designed to address problems that currently inhibit such investment. Some of the steps planned are the following:

—Supporting predevelopment activities to open up new acreage to industry on reasonable terms.

—Financing domestic infrastructure, which can make exploration and development investments more feasible.

—Participating in financing exploration projects through loans to governments or government companies for joint ventures where private companies are the operators or government programs where private contractors do the work. The Bank also is prepared to lend to local subsidiaries of international companies, with the full guarantee of the parent company, to help put together a large international venture.

—Participating in financing oil and gas development projects

so as to help create credible international financial packages. The
purpose of the Bank's oil and gas program is to expand opportunities for international investment. The Bank's technical assistance and its financial presence in these investments can improve
perceptions of political risk and provide additional assurance that
the terms of an agreement, once reached, will be carried out.

Coal might amount to 8 percent of the energy program. The
Bank estimates that progress here will be slow, because of the
lack of transportation infrastructure and poor geological information. Fuel wood development would amount to less than 5
percent of the program, but it is a generally neglected area that
has a very large impact on the poorest people in the world. It is
aimed at the low-income countries of Asia and Africa, where
firewood is still the primary cooking and heating fuel for 2 billion
people. Bank studies show that to maintain adequate supplies and
avoid further deforestation fuel wood planting would have to be
expanded to five times its current level. Since there is little
potential here for private investment, the necessary financing and
technical assistance will have to come from public sources—the
multilateral banks, the bilateral aid agencies, and the governments
concerned. The Bank will have to lead the way.

How might such an expanded program be financed? The
proposal for an energy affiliate for the Bank is one approach. Like
IDA, the work of an affiliate would be carried out by the Bank's
staff so that no new international bureaucracy would have to be
established, as is sometimes alleged. Its main advantages are that
it could facilitate the participation of capital surplus oil-exporting
countries in helping to finance an expanded energy program, and
it could generate additional financial leverage in Bank borrowing
on private markets. Since the United States has chosen not to
support the affiliate, at least for the time being, consideration of
this approach has to be deferred for all practical purposes. This
need be no loss in itself, since the main purpose served by an
affiliate—to enable the Bank to expand lending for energy—could
be accomplished in other ways.

Specifically, the member governments could each year authorize
an increase in the Bank's lending ceiling by an amount necessary
to finance the additional identifiable energy projects that meet the
Bank's lending standards but would otherwise be rejected for lack
of financing. Tom Clausen said last November that under present
lending limits, such a shortfall would amount to $1 billion in
1982, $2 billion in 1983, and almost $4 billion in 1984. At the
same time, the capital surplus oil-exporting countries might be

asked to cofinance additional Bank energy projects through their existing assistance agencies, or in other ways, in cooperation with an expanded Bank program. This would be particularly helpful in the poorest countries, where OPEC concessional financing could blend most effectively with the Bank's financing on market terms.

Lifting the lending ceiling each year to finance these additional energy projects would require that the question of the next capital increase for the Bank would have to be acted upon a year earlier, that is, in 1984 rather than 1985. In the meanwhile, no additional budgetary appropriations would be needed, and if it were agreed to increase capital subscriptions to the Bank in 1984, this probably could be done without a paid-in component, that is, without a further budgetary appropriation. Hence, budgetary considerations should not be a factor in deciding on the energy program. Nor is there any evident danger of a misallocation of capital. To the contrary, since the additional projects are likely to generate above-average economic rates of return, expanding the Bank's energy program would, if anything, contribute to a more effective use of capital worldwide.

In sum, there is a strong justification for an expanded role for the Bank in energy, now and for the foreseeable future. Energy has been catapulted into a priority sector. It is critical to the economic prospects of the oil-importing developing countries and on this count, among others, a potential drag on the industrial economies. The Bank is in a unique position to help in the adjustment process through technical assistance, policy advice, financial resources, and a general capacity to remove obstacles to investment—nonmarket obstacles, to be sure, but no less real for that. To preclude the Bank from playing its full role will be no service to anyone—not the oil-importing countries, not the industrial countries, and not the private energy sector.

## Summary of Comments by Fred L. Hartley

ENCOURAGING oil and gas investments requires assured and predictable rules of the game. This is critical. In recent years, industrial countries (Canada, Norway, and the United Kingdom) have been more likely to change the rules midstream, including taxation, than have developing countries.

The Bank has gone too far in its energy program. Oil and gas investment, from seismic work to exploration drilling to development, should be the responsibility of the private sector, which has the skills and the capital to do the job. Moreover, as demonstrated by the experience of Union Oil in Thailand and Indonesia, for example, the private foreign company also trains local technicians to take over from expatriate personnel. As long as private companies are prepared to accept the risks, there is no justification for using taxpayers' money for this purpose. Nor, for the same reasons, should the Bank support government enterprises in the oil and gas sector.

The World Bank can play an important role in two respects:

1. It can lend for infrastructure tied to oil and gas investments. In Thailand, Bank loans for a pipeline project made it possible to use the output of offshore gas discoveries. In the Philippines, Bank lending for an electric distribution system made it possible to gain the benefits of geothermal discoveries.

2. It can offer political risk insurance. World Bank insurance, as an extension of national political risk insurance, would give industry greater confidence in making investments and would give host countries a greater sense of responsibility, not just to the private investor, but to the international banking system as a whole.

Capital requirements for energy investments in the developing countries will be tremendous. Tying industry and the Bank together along the lines outlined above would maximize the possibilities for mobilizing such capital.

## Summary of Comments by Pedro-Pablo Kuczynski

IN CONSIDERING the Bank's role in energy, it is important to distinguish between oil and gas investments and electric power investments. Oil and gas is intimately dependent on private investment and will continue to be, even though state enterprises in some countries have a large role. These investments inevitably have a large foreign exchange context, for equipment and talent. This suggests that in considering its involvement the Bank should make sure a country exhausts the private investment possibilities available to it. Countries that keep the most promising acreage for national companies and offer the least promising acreage to foreign companies are going down the wrong road, particularly since the difference between the effective split in the two approaches, when account is taken of the costs of financing, technical assistance, and the rest, is not very great.

In electric power, the opposite situation exists. Public investment is predominant and in the case of hydroelectric power, the foreign exchange content is comparatively low. The Bank's involvement does not pose the risk of preempting private investment.

Energy, particularly oil and gas, is also complicated because it is so highly charged politically. The Bank has the potential to ease these obstacles. For example, an increase in the domestic price of gasoline, which may be long overdue on economic grounds, will subject a government to the political charge that it is acting on behalf of the domestic oil producers, which are foreign-owned companies. Similarly, there is a tendency in negotiating with foreign companies on oil and gas concessions to become preoccupied with squeezing the last drop out of an agreement, partly to protect the political flanks of the negotiating officials, at the cost of long delays in the start of drilling or of even getting the project under way at all. What is needed is a change in philosophy in these countries to get the priorities right. The Bank, with all its lines to governments, through loans and technical assistance, and because of its reputation for objectivity, could help to bring this about.

On the question raised by Hartley of whether the Bank should be engaged in seismic work, there is merit in having an inventory of basic oil information in every country that has a geophysical potential for oil and gas.

The energy affiliate concept might best be thought of as a means of promoting private-sector investments through offering loan guarantees and providing technical advice—in effect, education about normal practices and standards in the oil and gas business. This would reduce or eliminate some of the political myths that are obstacles to the negotiation of agreements.

## Summary of Comments by Maurice F. Strong

THE BANK'S role is indispensable to generating a substantial increase in energy investment in the developing world. In many instances, it is the only game in town. Its leadership and intellectual capacity, which are a prime legacy of the McNamara era, can be a major asset in building a creative and effective partnership between public and private capital. To do this, it must itself be able to supply funds.

Some forty developing countries are believed to have significant oil and gas potential. Increased exploration activity is the key to realizing this potential. The Bank is already mounting an effective program in preexploration activities. It is also willing to participate in financing infrastructure and development, should oil or gas be discovered. Both programs improve the climate for exploration.

In exploration itself, the Bank should play a leadership and catalytic role, directed toward facilitating, encouraging, and supporting private-sector and other sources of financing. Bank funds are needed, but on a comparatively small scale, to be used, in effect, to provide risk insurance for other investors. Examples include the following:

—Mitigating political risks, either through creation of a new insurance mechanism, or more informally by virtue of the Bank's leadership and presence in oil exploration projects, which provides the necessary confidence for cofinancing by others.

—The major companies, by operating in a number of countries, can spread the exploration and political risks much more in accord with actuarial probabilities. Smaller and less experienced investors cannot do this. The Bank, by helping to create new risk-spreading mechanisms, such as drilling funds and exploration consortia, could help to tap additional sources of funds for exploration drilling and increase the total level of exploration activity.

We should recognize that national oil companies—in oil-exporting countries, industrial countries, and oil-importing developing countries—are, and will be, major factors in oil and gas, whether we like it or not. They are an important source of exploration capital, but some do not have the expertise or capacity as yet to conduct programs on a scale large enough for risk diversification. Here, too, new Bank mechanisms and leadership could help.

The IFC also has an impressive potential to expand its role in this area. Here again the purpose is catalytic, to expand financial flows from a variety of sources.

Altogether, at least $1 billion a year for the next three or four years would be a realistic estimate of new exploration funds that would be provided by consortium groups like my company, the International Energy Development Corporation, in response to a concerted extension of the World Bank's leadership function in oil and gas exploration.

## General Discussion

THEODORE H. MORAN of Georgetown University said that his studies of the Bank's oil and gas program showed the following:

—In most cases the Bank has in fact acted as a catalyst to the private sector.

—Preexploration activities (which the Bank terms exploration promotion) have been the most successful up to now. This consists of financing seismic work and providing technical advice to countries about creating a feasible legal framework for negotiating agreements and about normal industry practices. This work has helped to open up acreage to competitive bidding by the international industry and facilitated the negotiation of exploration agreements with private firms.

—The demand for Bank financing for development of oil and gas discoveries seems to be much less than might be expected, despite the general agreement in the discussion on the need for political risk insurance. He asked why this was so.

Hartley, in response to this last point, said such financing was an entrepreneurial function that the private sector was, and should be, prepared to accept.

MacLaury wondered whether the discussion was becoming too dichotomized as to whether the World Bank had a role in energy or not. There seems to be general agreement on its insurance role. Beyond that, there clearly is disagreement on the question raised at the beginning of the discussion: would additional bank lending in energy crowd out private-sector investments or serve as seed capital to encourage additional private investment?

Robert V. Roosa of Brown Brothers Harriman asked why one should not think of the Bank, or the IFC, or an energy affiliate of the Bank as a minority participant in an oil and gas exploration or development project, in the same way as it is normal industry practice for a number of private companies to join in a consortium for such investments. The Bank could be a useful participant in such risk-sharing joint ventures in instances where its contribution, in addition to financing, was knowledge of the economy and local institutions and a unique understanding of economic capacities, requirements, and constraints in the country concerned.

Khelil said the discussion had concentrated too much on oil and gas, which is by far the smaller part of the Bank's energy program. The problem was that without an increase in lending capacity, the Bank could not increase its lending for all forms of energy without cutting back on projects in agriculture and construction. That is where the creation of an energy affiliate could help, by increasing the resources available for energy lending without cutting other high-priority projects. That is why the capital surplus oil-exporting countries and the oil-importing developing countries have been impatient about the creation of an energy affiliate.

Edwin Deagle, director of international relations for the Rocke-feller Foundation, said that of the $70 billion to $80 billion in financing McNamara estimated was needed for structural adjust-ment in the oil-importing developing countries, $15 billion applied to sixty-nine small, low-income, oil-importing countries plus India and the Philippines. For these countries, cost-effective lending was needed across the board, not simply for energy alone. Some of the hard-hit countries had little in the way of energy resources but would have to increase their earning capacity, through export expansion, to pay for oil imports.

Garcia-Parra said that to describe Bank loans as representing the use of taxpayers' money is misleading. Bank funds are loaned at interest rates virtually equal to the market and recently may have been exceeding the market, if all costs are included. (IDA credits, on the other hand, which go only to the poorest countries, are interest free and may fairly be described as taxpayers' money.) Moreover, bank resources for lending are obtained almost entirely from borrowing on private capital markets, not from budgetary appropriations.

Fried, in summing up, emphasized the importance of energy investments other than oil and gas, which are two-thirds of the Bank's program. Bank projects in electric power and other energy areas attract private capital in the form of foreign supplier credits and commercial bank loans. They reduce the need for future oil imports and represent necessary structural adjustment. Nonethe-less, the Bank will not be able to finance some of these projects, even though they are expected to have high economic rates of return, unless it has additional lending authority.

In the oil and gas sector the most numerous Bank projects so far are for preexploration activities, whose objective is to open up acreage more quickly to competitive bidding. Most discussants here would agree these projects will facilitate private-sector in-volvement.

In exploration itself (as distinct from appraisal drilling), the Bank has been involved in only a handful of projects, usually where there has been no interest on the part of private companies but the government, on the basis of reasonably promising geo-logical data, wishes to proceed. Even in these cases, the Bank seeks to stimulate the interest of the private sector by sponsoring new activity in the area. Generally, the Bank's policy in exploration is to exhaust private-sector possibilities first, just as Kuczynski has recommended, or to become involved in projects at the request of private companies, who seek such involvement as a type of political risk insurance.

The question has been raised as to why companies have not expressed greater interest in Bank financing for developing oil and gas discoveries. Bank projects to help finance infrastructure tied to oil and gas development, which a number of companies have requested, fit this definition. It is well to remember, moreover, that the oil and gas program is comparatively new and lead times are long. If it turns out that there is no need for Bank involvement in development projects, which could require large amounts of funds, the Bank as a residual lender should be happy to bow out.

# The Future Role
# of the World Bank Group

R. T. McNAMAR

WE REGARD the World Bank Group as an integral component of the Reagan administration's overall approach to international economics. The Bank will be severely tested in the future, both in the capital markets and in the economic realities of third world countries.

The Bank has already demonstrated its flexibility in adapting its program to different recipients from its founding in 1946 until today. From 1945 to 1960 the Bank's efforts were focused on postwar reconstruction, with development interests picking up sharply in the latter part of the period. The 1960s saw the emergence of third world efforts. The Bank's efforts were exclusively in developing countries and largely in infrastructure projects. IDA began to operate on a substantial scale during this period.

Despite major international economic disruptions, the period from 1970 to 1980 saw a growth in multilateral aid and a reorientation of lending toward directly aiding the rural poor. In the aftermath of the oil shocks of 1973–74 and 1979–80, the private banking sector moved into a major role as the provider of the developing countries' external finance. Official finance became increasingly constrained at the end of this period.

As to the 1980s, where do we go from here? That is what I would like to talk about.

*Emphasis on domestic savings and foreign trade*

From the economic perspective, there are several important facts that influence the U.S. view of the economic development process. First, for oil-importing developing countries, domestic capital still provides the bedrock for most economic growth. Second, foreign capital finances only one-seventh of the total investment. Official development aid provides only about 4 percent of all foreign exchange available to oil-importing developing countries. Gross exports are the largest source of such foreign exchange, providing approximately 83 percent of the total.

These figures show that to focus solely on official development aid, as is the case in many discussions of development, is

38

analytically inadequate. Aid is important for many of the poorest countries with limited exports and little access to funds in commercial terms, to be sure. However, resisting protectionism and ensuring access to markets is of far more importance to developing countries as a whole. The issues of protectionism and market access should receive more prominence in the discussion of economic development.

*Benefits of a strong U.S. economy*

In external capital flows, the United States is an important partner in the developing countries' economic growth process. On the export side, we know the United States is the largest market for LDC [less developed countries] exports. In 1979, for example, the United States obtained a larger share, 23 percent, of its imports from oil-importing developing countries than did any other industrialized country.

The United States buys over 50 percent of all oil-importing developing countries' exports of manufactured goods. To put the importance of the U.S. market in perspective, developing countries' earnings from exports to the United States are double the amount of foreign aid from all the industrialized countries. A strong U.S. economy, therefore, means growing export markets for the LDCs. Indeed, as these figures indicate, the greatest contribution the United States can make to developing countries is to have sustained noninflationary growth in its own economy.

With respect to financial flows, U.S. banks are important intermediaries for financial resources: approximately 40 percent of the developing country loans from commercial banks are owed to U.S. banks or their branches and affiliates.

Another way noninflationary growth in the United States helps the developing world is in its impact on interest rates and debt service. Much of the debt owed by developing countries is at floating rates. Each 1 percentage point decline in interest rates results in about a $1 billion reduction in developing country debt service. This means that the immediate benefits of a 6 percentage point drop in interest rates would be virtually equal to U.S. official development assistance. In fact, the fall from last summer's high rate of around 19.5 percent has eased developing country debt service by $5 billion, or approximately two-thirds of recent U.S. official development assistance levels.

Finally, the United States remains the largest contributor of official development assistance. Funds derived from export earnings and from reduced debt service help to avoid what can be called the development dilemma, the existing paradox in aid programs. We suggest that this is the dilemma: increased aid increases industrial countries' budget deficits at a time when their deficits already are considered to be too large. Similarly, measures to increase liquidity, such as SDR [special drawing rights] allocations, increase international liquidity at a time when liquidity is already excessive. The tendency has been to monetize the larger deficits, which along with the increased SDR liquidity increases inflation and therefore interest rates. The higher interest rates increase the debt service burden to the LDCs and so the cycle is repeated. The result is to worsen conditions in developing countries' export markets and, in effect, at some point, the short-term "fixes" of increased aid and increased liquidity may be self-defeating in the long run.

Of course, the contribution of sustained noninflationary growth in the United States also allows us to provide security assistance and a military umbrella, assuring the peace and stability that is necessary for economic development. Indeed, those who criticize the United States for low development assistance should recognize the assistance we provide to development through the security umbrella as well.

Finally, those who assert that the United States has been "disgraceful" in its support of multilateral institutions, I point out two facts. First, if our share of aid has dropped from the high watermark of the Marshall Plan days, our share of the world GNP has also dropped from 42 percent in 1950 to 21 percent in 1980. Second, the United States was the strongest supporter of the World Bank and IMF at the recent Cancún summit. The Reagan administration stands second to none in support of the multilateral development banks.

To sum up, in order to address what I believe is the current development dilemma, the United States must achieve sustained noninflationary growth, which in turn can provide increased export earnings and reduced debt service to developing countries.

***The development continuum***

There is a development capital continuum in which it is useful to view the World Bank and the development effort. At the bottom, or at the extreme of the continuum, are the poorest countries, and these developing countries receive the most concessional aid, through IDA, for example, with very little nonconcessional financing.

As they move along the continuum, they reach progressive stages. First, they become blend countries receiving IBRD financing. Eventually, cofinancing with private sources gradually becomes the largest component of their external flows. Such cofinancing can occur with the development banks' regular lending as well as with the International Finance Corporation. Finally, at the graduation stage, official lending, which by then is a very small component, ceases entirely. Indeed, such countries can become providers of capital for the development efforts of others.

That is the continuum through which economic development operates, in my judgment. World Bank Group lending should be seen in this continuum and judged against its ability to assist borrowers in moving through the continuum.

Let me talk first about concessional assistance. Everyone must recognize the political environment in which we operate, with the limited prospects for new expanded aid initiatives and the congressional difficulties involved in keeping aid at current levels. In this context we consider congressional authorization of IDA funds at the negotiated levels a major victory for the Reagan administration. We also count as a success the fact that we have got Congress to pass the first foreign assistance appropriations bill since 1978.

At present we eagerly await the specifics of the promised Bank initiative regarding the repackaging of IDA financing. The new proposal must be economically sound. It must be responsive to IDA's critics or refute them with convincing analysis, not hollow rhetoric. The key issues which I believe must be faced in any proposal for IDA are the length of maturities, including possible acceleration of repayment schedules; fees and rates charged; and the conditionality and the relationship to blend lending.

We cannot expect larger and larger replenishments for concessional financing. The political and economic realities will not permit it. The Reagan administration will not make popular, convenient commitments that we know we cannot get through Congress. Nor will we make commitments our successors will find difficult or impossible to get through Congress. While it might be appealing in the short term to do so, it would be disingenuous to create false expectations. We wish to avoid that.

Let me turn now to the blend countries. The maturation of blend countries into the IBRD must be pursued substantially and consistently. Traditional treatment of particular countries must be rethought in light of current realities. For example, if a country can devote scarce resources to wasteful domestic programs, can it really be viewed as a major contender for concessional lending?

Let us talk about hard lending. With regard to IBRD hard lending, I might briefly mention that the general capital increase authorization legislation has been signed by the president, as has the appropriation for the first U.S. subscription of $109.7 million of paid-in capital and the accompanying callable capital. We would like to see all blend countries that are in a satisfactory balance of payments position move rapidly into IBRD-only lending.

With this greater dependence on the IBRD, however, I must note with concern the Bank's past practice of making fixed-rate commitments. We will await with interest the coming Bank analysis of floating rates and variable terms, which have become common in other financial institutions. We would like to emphasize, however, the importance of thoroughly analyzing and understanding the problem.

We do not want a solution in what I would regard as the energy affiliate mode. Bluntly put, this is an area that the private sector can and will adequately serve. The energy affiliate would simply substitute less expensive public development capital for available private capital. Indeed, the Bank is meeting the challenge through expanded energy lending within its budgetary limitation. We strongly support this change in policy.

*Stimulating private capital flows*

In considering new lending initiatives, the Bank should give greater weight to the appropriate policy response by recipients and the catalytic effect on non-Bank resource flows. Indeed, the Bank, and development policy in general, must place greater focus on the generation of nonaid capital if it is to adequately serve the needs of developing countries.

To that end, let me talk about cofinancing, a potentially major segment of the development continuum. The role of catalyzing private financial flows is not something new. Article I of the Bank's charter specifically calls for the Bank to "promote private foreign investments by means of guarantees or participation in loans and other investments made by private investors."

The view that the MDBs [multilateral development banks] must become more active financial catalysts for private capital flows in the years ahead is shared by Tom Clausen, who stated this in his inaugural speech at the World Bank–International Monetary Fund meeting last fall. He said: "The private sector particularly represents an immense potential source of investment capital and, we, the Bank, will seek to increase substantially the level of private cofinancing in the next several years."

Of course, cofinancing is not something new. Substantial progress to involve the private commercial banks in the activities of the MDBs began under Bob McNamara's presidency and is continuing.

The MDBs have instituted active programs to involve commercial banks in greater cofinancing. In 1976 the World Bank had five projects out of seventy-three that were cofinanced with private as opposed to public institutions, accounting for approximately $272 million from the private sector. By 1981, eighteen of seventy-nine cofinanced projects involved commercial banks, so that private cofinancing was $1.7 billion. By way of perspective, this $1.7 billion exceeds the total lending of the Asian Development Bank and comes close to matching the lending volume of the Inter-American Development Bank in its most recent fiscal years. In other words, right now cofinancing is a major and growing source of development assistance. We applaud this trend and hope to see it continue.

Given the compelling logic and budgetary pressures toward growth of private cofinancing, it seems almost inevitable that cofinancing will expand. This expansion is not inevitable, however. Wanting to make it happen will not make it happen. In our view, at least, three things should take place if we are actually to fulfill the potential that is there. First, cofinancing must be more actively marketed by the development banks themselves. Second, the cofinancing package must be made more attractive to the private banks, and finally, regulatory concerns must be addressed.

In terms of marketing the cofinancing activities more actively, this is the primary responsibility of the development banks' management. The number of commercial banks involved in this activity must be expanded. To date, thirty-six U.S. commercial banks have participated in World Bank cofinanced projects. This is nearly one-third of all banks worldwide that have participated, but that total must be increased substantially.

In order to expand private cofinancing, the cofinancing package may have to be made more attractive. Any or all of the following may prove necessary.

Project information will need to be shared throughout the life of the project, not just at the beginning. MDB-borrower dialogue must include cofinancing as a priority item.

Why should not those countries approaching the IBRD graduation threshold be expected to have an increasingly larger percentage of their borrowings represented by cofinancing? Is that not an attractive policy for the bank to evaluate and consider adopting? The World Bank will, in fact, shortly issue a board paper on revisions in its graduation policy. We hope the Bank will strongly consider making the role of cofinancing more explicit in its delineation of graduation and maturation stages.

Cross-default clauses may have to be made mandatory. New

cofinancing instruments and techniques may be necessary. The Bank is considering a scheme whereby certain new loans will contain two parts—an "A" loan funded exclusively by the IBRD and a "B" loan normally funded by private lenders at market rates, but structured so it could include IBRD funds as well to provide added security and stretch maturities. We also believe that the IFC, with its proven private-sector track record, can be helpful to the Bank in these efforts.

Of course, the existing regulatory environment is of considerable importance in this whole area of private cofinancing. We are all aware of the 10 percent of capital limit in commercial bank lending to a single borrower, as stipulated by law. But how this 10 percent limit is interpreted by the comptroller of the currency has implications for the growth of cofinancing. I have asked the new comptroller of the currency to reexamine the present interpretation when it comes to cofinanced loans with multilateral development banks. Legislative changes also may be appropriate and will be considered.

Overseas the same reconsideration is occurring, and foreign bank supervisory bodies are reviewing their treatment of cofinancing. This could also increase the private capital the World Bank could attract to its projects. In this regard the Bank of England's views on cofinanced loans are relevant. It takes the position that the inclusion of more cofinanced loans in a bank's asset portfolio could lead to a perception on the part of supervisors that the bank had lowered the overall risk in its lending, and such a development would influence their assessment of the extent to which the bank could prudently expand its lending further.

I also note the change made by the Amsterdam-Rotterdam Bank, to use a separate evaluation for cofinanced loans with multilateral development institutions, wholly outside the country ceilings ordinarily used by the Bank.

The lesser credit risk and the increased security with respect to political uncertainties and the quality of projects were felt to justify this action. Those bankers who complain about the spreads of cofinanced loans being too thin would do well to take a lesson from their Dutch and Japanese colleagues, especially since the lower spreads are very consistent with modern portfolio theory.

In fact, we believe that the financial markets do work, and since there is less risk on an MDB cofinanced loan, the spreads may be appropriately smaller. Moreover, if loans cofinanced with the World Bank and other multilaterals are much less subject to rescheduling and default than other commercial bank loans, supervisory evaluations should reflect this. We intend to ask the relevant regulators in the United States to consider this action.

The IFC is another important vehicle for cofinancing. Last year, for example, nearly half of the IFC's $180 million in equity and loan commitments were associated with IFC syndications, involving over fifty financial institutions.

In looking to the Bank to increase its catalytic role and the leveraging of its financial resources, I would like to raise the possibility of a larger relative role for the IFC. As some of you know, the United States has been talking with the IFC informally and has some ideas on its future directions. Among these are that the IFC should concentrate its activities more directly on those areas of comparative advantage. It should undertake projects where it has the greatest economic and development impact. It should seek ways to increase its types of financial activities either on its own or in concert with other financial institutions.

There are four specific areas where the IFC possesses substantial advantage, in our judgment.

—First, the development of capital markets primarily through technical assistance is an essential IFC activity that could be expanded.

—The IFC has a singular capability of fashioning an impressive financial package that would give leverage to IFC dollars.

—Traditionally, its lending and equity programs have focused on private-sector market-oriented industrial activities, which should be viewed as an increased area of specialization.

—The IFC is in an unique position to assist the LDCs in developing more efficient industrial policies, which are indispensable in stimulating private-capital projects.

Finally, while it is too early to tell whether the IFC or the Bank will be the lead institution, I would like at this point to endorse in principle the investment insurance scheme mentioned by President Clausen. We look forward to seeing specific proposals at an appropriate time.

**Graduation**

Our development continuum, which began with concessional financing, ends with graduation from the Bank. Greater movement of countries through the development continuum of necessity involves an increased graduation effort.

As private flows increase, whether through cofinancing or other forms, scarce aid resources should be focused increasingly on the most deserving. The winners in the competition for limited funds must be the poorest in income terms and those which promise and deliver the best performance.

In our view, there is no virtue in providing Bank funds to countries that do not need aid. All present and future loans should be evaluated in this light. Of course, the ultimate goal of the Bank is for countries to become self-sufficient and independent so that they do not need official external capital. Indeed, over its history a number of earlier borrowers of the Bank have achieved this status.

In conclusion, as you know, when we came into office we did a policy assessment of multilateral development banks. The basis for what I have said today is that assessment.[1] We believe that the assessment provides a sound analytical basis and justification for continued strong U.S. support for all the MDBs, including the World Bank Group.

The Bank Group has been the critical means for effective policy reform in the developing world. In the future, it will increase its critical role as a catalyst for private projects.

As the Bank changes, the United States will enthusiastically participate in its evolutionary process of building a consensus for new directions.

It is important that the World Bank, as well as other international financial institutions, be protected against disruptive changes that would shake the confidence of the private investors.

President Reagan said at the last Bank-Fund meeting: "We strongly support the World Bank and because of our strong support we feel a special responsibility to provide constructive suggestions to make it more effective.

"We believe the suggestions will permit it to generate increased funds for development and to support the efforts developing countries are making to strengthen their own economies."

I hope you will take these ideas I have presented today in that spirit. The Reagan administration strongly supports the World Bank and will continue to do so, given leadership and policy changes we foresee in its future.

1. The Treasury Department published this assessment in February 1982: *United States Participation in the Multilateral Development Banks in the 1980s* (Government Printing Office, 1982).

# The Roles of Multilateral and Bilateral Aid

DAVID ROCKEFELLER

I HAVE been asked to summarize the various arguments—pro and con—with respect to both bilateral and multilateral aid to developing nations. This is a task I approach with a certain sense of déjà vu since I was asked some fourteen years ago to participate in a similar review as a member of President Johnson's General Advisory Committee on Foreign Assistance Programs, chaired by Jim Perkins.

Interestingly, and unfortunately, many of our conclusions in 1968 continue to be relevant in 1982. The report began with our conviction that sound and substantial development assistance was in the basic interest of the United States, and went on to note: "Yet in America today a mood of malaise and withdrawal is enfeebling U.S. development assistance efforts."

The major financial and emotional stumbling block at that time was, of course, the war in Vietnam. Today, that war is behind us, but domestic economic problems pose similar constraints in terms of both financial ability and national will.

Over the past year, the question of foreign assistance has come very much to the foreground again as a result of the Brandt Commission report, the debate over the "new international economic order," the emphasis of the new administration on bilateral and private-sector approaches as opposed to multilateral approaches, and the discussions of these issues which took place in Cancún.

Once again, I have become more involved personally through my work with such groups as the U.S. Business Committee on Jamaica and the new Americas Society. I have urged the creation of a high-level private sector task force to review the whole question of the self-interest of the United States in regard to its relations with the so-called third world.

*U.S. self-interest and development assistance in general*

The Perkins Commission in 1968 was countering a strong resistance in the nation and in Congress against development assistance in general. Congress had sharply cut back aid funds for fiscal years 1968 and 1969, and we were urging a return at least to the

47

levels of 1963–67, when aid averaged about 0.75 percent of U.S. GNP. When our report was written, U.S. aid had dropped to 0.35 percent. The long-term impact of our report can be seen in the fact that current U.S. aid has not only *not increased* as a percentage of GNP, but actually *declined* further to a mere 0.23 percent in 1978. Whereas the United States was once preeminent in foreign assistance, we now lag behind twelve other Western nations when measured by the percentage of GNP contributed. And the capital surplus oil-producing nations are in another league entirely, with Kuwait, for example, now dedicating some 4 percent of its GNP to foreign assistance, and in some past years twice that percentage.

Three questions we felt compelled to respond to in 1968 are still being asked today. First was whether or not the United States could afford development assistance. Our response was then, and I support it even more strongly at this time, that we cannot afford *not* to assist developing nations. For reasons of political stability, because of economic interests involving trade and investment, and out of moral and humanitarian concerns, aid to developing nations has a legitimate claim on the funds provided our government by the American taxpayer. The amounts required are relatively small, and the returns in terms of global stability and human and economic progress are great.

A second question was whether development assistance could be effective. The answer then and now, I believe, is affirmative based on the number of nations that have been helped to achieve self-sustaining economic progress. In 1968, we pointed to examples such as Israel, Taiwan, Greece, Turkey, and Korea. Today, the list is far longer. More recent examples include Brazil, Malaysia, and Thailand, and even Bangladesh is now nearly self-sufficient in agriculture.

The third question was whether development assistance could be managed soundly. We concluded that the programs of the Agency for International Development and the World Bank were indeed well managed and getting better with experience. The records of these agencies and the regional banks in the fourteen years since seem to me to underscore the validity of this conclusion. By and large, programs administered both by multilateral agencies and bilateral initiatives have produced good results.

An issue we barely touched on in 1968 was the overall economic importance of the prosperity of the developing nations to our own well-being. This has come to have enormous significance today. The developing nations now provide a larger *export* market than all the developed nations put together, excluding only Canada. And U.S. exports to these nations between 1973 and 1979 grew at an average annual rate of 20 percent, compared with a rate of 15 percent to industrialized countries. On the *import* side, developing nations supply not only vital oil and strategic raw materials, but also lower-priced consumer goods, which help combat inflation.

Finally, I would suggest that even the moral and humanitarian aspects of aid cannot be disassociated from U.S. self-interest. Our country was built on Judeo-Christian ethical principles, which taught us to be concerned with the well-being of our fellow man. As Bob McNamara has stated so poignantly over the years, we cannot ignore the fact that nearly 1 billion people on this earth live today below the poverty line. They rightfully have a claim on our sympathy and our pocketbooks. Assistance to help countries with the lowest standard of living generally must come from multilateral sources or direct bilateral government aid. Clearly, IDA has an especially important role to play and thus our prompt and ample funding of IDA replenishment is essential.

I dwell on the overall issues of the validity and self-interest of assistance for a reason. Now, as in 1968, it is imperative that there be a greater national consensus about the importance and value of our providing help to developing nations. Without this, it will be impossible to arrive at a reasonable overall agreement as to how much the United States can and should spend. Such agreement, it seems to me, is in a sense a precondition to discussions of the relative merits of various forms of aid. Once a level is agreed upon, then we can figure out how to get the greatest relative impact in terms of the human condition and our own longer-term self-interest.

***Pros and cons of bilateral and multilateral assistance***    It might help to very briefly list some of the pros and cons I frequently hear about the relative merits of bilateral and multilateral aid.

First of all are the bilateral pros:
—ability to focus on politically congenial nations (such as Jamaica);
—ability to focus geographically (such as the Caribbean Basin);
—ability to focus programmatically (such as family planning);
—ability to link closely to private efforts on a project-by-project basis.

The cons of bilateral aid are:
—limited reach—only one country at a time;

—lack of multiplier effect (we don't get the benefits of the help of other nations);
—danger of becoming identified with unsavory governments with resulting resentment by local population;
—possible "colonialist" interpretation;
—reduced flexibility through congressional earmarking;
—resentment of other countries not receiving bilateral aid from us.

Now, the multilateral pros:
—multiplier effect;
—relative political neutrality and ability to insist on sound development practices;
—broad impact;
—shared "ownership";
—greater continuity and consistency.

And last, the drawbacks of multilateral aid:
—lack of U.S. control (ideological, geographic and programmatic);
—difficulty of tailoring for private involvement on case-by-case basis.

I personally believe the current administration's focus on U.S. self-interest in looking at bilateral assistance and on private-sector involvement is realistic and refreshing. At the same time, our self-interest also requires that we not go to extremes and ignore the importance of multilateral assistance as well. What is needed, to my mind, is not the abandonment of one form of aid or another but rather a sharper emphasis on the measurement of results. What works? What doesn't work? What is or is not in our own broadly defined self-interest? Finally, what can we afford to do in such a manner that both we and the recipients find acceptable?

It also might be useful to address a few key specific issues with respect to both multilateral and bilateral approaches. On the multilateral side, for instance, there are increasing calls among developing nations for the IMF to become involved in social lending. I am personally concerned about how far in this direction this can go without subverting the vital role of the IMF as our economic policeman. Another key issue is the gearing ratio of the World Bank, which the Brandt Commission recommended be increased from 1 to 1 to 2 to 1, thereby raising its borrowing capacity to $160 billion. While I am not sure that an immediate doubling of the ratio would be prudent, I do believe that the World Bank's successful track record fully justifies a progressive increase of the present ratio over the next few years. Unquestionably, World Bank and IMF involvement in a developing country today gives added confidence to the private commercial banks, whose role in recycling petrodollars to the third world has been of crucial importance in recent years.

On the bilateral side, two issues come to mind for further exploration. One is the question of ongoing desirability of the "basic human needs" provision attached to aid under the Foreign Assistance Act. If we are going to emphasize private-sector economic development, it seems to me that this provision needs some change and/or clarification. The second issue relates to the extent to which human rights considerations should influence our aid policy and programs. I think a more realistic and balanced approach is needed here as well, with careful assessment on a case-by-case basis. Arbitrary and inflexible standards should not be applied. Goals and a positive direction must be pursued, but each situation must be judged in its geographic and historical context.

**The role of the private sector**

Since the administration has emphasized the role of the private sector in international development, I thought I might conclude my own remarks with a few lessons we have learned in this area from the work of the U.S. Business Committee on Jamaica:

—Pure private investment in the more traditional sense will not do the trick by itself, especially in the short run. Continued governmental assistance is vital in the short term, and new forms of public and private involvement and cooperation must be created for the longer term.

—Money is only a small part of the challenge. Training and technical assistance also are critical. In addition, good organizational planning and the capacity for swift decisionmaking can be the difference between success and failure in many cases.

—Smaller businesses have a critical role to play. While discussions of private international development tend to revolve around large multinational corporations, smaller corporations have resources and expertise that are too often overlooked. Involving such corporations to a greater degree is an important committee objective.

—The bilateral approach advocated by the U.S. government seems to work well in Jamaica since it can be targeted on a case-by-case basis, but there also is a very important ongoing role for multilateral strategies with respect to balance of payments problems, capital availability, and trade. Furthermore, there is a place, heretofore little explored, for multilateral cooperation within the private sector.

—Even with intense private-sector involvement and enthusiastic receptivity to such involvement on the part of the host country, tangible development in terms of new jobs and economic growth does not take place overnight. Without patience and perseverance on all sides, progress will be slight. I mention this point because expectations quickly rise; when results are not achieved quickly, disillusionment sets in.

The question of a more direct role of the private sector in international development is complex and involves many other issues as well. For instance, Tom Clausen has raised the issue of private cofinancing with the World Bank, and I certainly agree with him on the potential there. I believe it is an idea which should be pursued aggressively.

The fact is that the subject of private-sector involvement and the relative effectiveness of different public aid mechanisms deserves a more thorough study, within the context of U.S. self-interest, than it has received to date. Many of the conditions and problems are similar to those that existed in 1968, but the global context has changed considerably. I think it is timely that a solid, overall, action-oriented review of options be undertaken now so that fourteen years hence—in 1996—there is not again the same sense of déjà vu I feel today.

## Summary of Comments by Warren M. Christopher

MULTILATERAL aid has many advantages, as cited by David Rockefeller. However bilateral aid serves important foreign policy purposes, for example, in making possible the Camp David peace process. It is also sometimes essential on economic grounds, when multilateral aid is not sufficient to meet the need—as in the case of Turkey—or in conveying technological assistance that comes more effectively through bilateral than through multilateral channels. It also serves security purposes, for example, in facilitating the Philippine base negotiations.

Bilateral aid can be decided and furnished more quickly than multilateral aid, which can be critical in an emergency or where flexibility is essential. Nor does it follow that bilateral aid is unilateral, thus tending to isolate the United States politically; bilateral aid can be provided through consortia such as that organized by Germany for Turkey or those the World Bank organizes for various developing countries. This type of multilateralism is likely to increase in the future. Furthermore, bilateral aid, because of its evident political and economic benefits to the United States, meets with congressional favor more readily than does multilateral aid, and so helps to carry the total foreign aid appropriation.

Another consideration is that bilateral economic aid is a more attractive means of forging links with developing countries than supplying them with growing quantities of sophisticated weapons they neither need nor can use. A strong program of bilateral economic aid provides an opportunity to reserve military aid for the few instances where it is necessary.

Multilateral aid programs must go forward, but from a political, economic, and even developmental standpoint, a strong case exists for mounting a properly mutually supportive balance between bilateral and multilateral aid.

## Summary of Comments by C. Fred Bergsten

BOTH BILATERAL and multilateral aid are needed in a balanced program, but, despite current criticisms in the United States, the comparative case for multilateral aid is all the stronger at a time of budgetary stringency. These criticisms are that it costs too much, does not effectively support U.S. foreign policy, promotes the wrong economic policies, and generally operates without U.S. influence. Each of these criticisms is wrong; indeed, the reverse is true.

Multilateral aid is clearly the least-cost form of economic assistance because it is based on burden sharing among nations and on leveraging public funds with capital from private markets. In concessional aid, every dollar of U.S. contributions to IDA is matched by three dollars from other countries. For the World Bank's hard lending, every dollar invested by the United States in paid-in capital subscriptions generates seventy dollars in World Bank loans. When account is taken of the stimulus given to commercial bank lending, the leverage is even greater. For the same reason, U.S. exports generated from World Bank loans are a large multiple of the budget money we put in. Thus at a time of budgetary stringency, the case for multilateral aid is stronger than ever. Cuts in U.S. support, such as reduced appropriations for IDA, waste these multiplier effects just when they are needed most.

A prime example at present is Central America and the Caribbean. Sharp increases are needed in concessional assistance to that area. Yet the administration apparently is envisaging a cut of over 70 percent (from $175 million to $50 million) in the U.S. pledge to the Fund for Special Operations of the Inter-American Development Bank, most of whose funds go to that area. Other donors can be expected to cut back proportionately. There is no way that U.S. bilateral aid will bridge this difference.

Bilateral aid is probably not an effective way of exercising political influence, except in a very few cases where that aid can be concentrated in large amounts. Our procedures for allocating and administering bilateral aid are too slow and cumbersome; the alternative sources of finance to the recipients are too great; and linkages among issues are too complex.

In contrast, the World Bank has the analytical competence, the technical skills, the financial resources, and the political acceptability to promote sound economic policies in developing countries; this strongly advances U.S. foreign policy interests. Instead of encouraging socialism, as is sometimes alleged, the Bank has been the most consistent and strongest exponent of market-oriented policies in the developing world. Bank projects typically show economic rates of return of 15 percent to 20 percent.

Obviously, the United States does not control the Bank; if it did, it would not gain the large burden-sharing and multiplier benefits now enjoyed. On the other hand, U.S. influence is very great; there is no major issue in Bank policies where U.S. objectives have not been successfully pursued. In this connection, the administration cannot bring about the operating changes it wants and at the same time reduce its financial support for the Bank. These two goals are mutually exclusive, since our influence in this institution depends on our financial support.

## General Discussion

DAVID NEWSOM, former undersecretary of state, stressed the role of the World Bank in organizing consortia that brought both bilateral and multilateral aid donors to a particular country together. If these consortia are to succeed, substantial U.S. bilateral aid is essential, he argued; otherwise other countries will not follow suit.

Hartley asked if aid to China should be contingent on its favoring private investment. Bergsten said that the same rules should be applied there as elsewhere. Walker stressed the importance of price mechanisms to ensure that resources will be used effectively.

Owen commended the administration for increasingly focusing bilateral development aid on scientific and technological cooperation with developing countries, leaving the task of transferring large resources for development purposes to these countries to the multilateral development banks. In this way, bilateral and multilateral aid can effectively complement each other.

John Sewell, president of the Overseas Development Council, said that the United States has a growing stake in the economic development of the third world and that private capital flows to these countries now far exceed public flows. It is important, therefore, to think hard about how these private flows can be increased and not to concentrate excessively on public flows, important though they are. He commended Rockefeller's proposal for a private study of U.S. interests in economic development and how they can best be pursued.

A participant asked Christopher how he could reconcile the United States persuading the World Bank to cut off multilateral aid to Vietnam while continuing bilateral aid to the junta in El Salvador. Christopher explained that the Vietnam cutoff was due to a specific congressional mandate, and that economic aid was the most sensible way of expressing our support for the government of El Salvador.

Leland said our interest in the developing countries is a security interest and that this interest is advanced by their improved well-being. He said that the United States has substantial influence in the multilateral development banks, mostly because other industrial countries share our views on using the banks' resources effectively, and these banks have substantial influence in developing countries. There is no reason to be ashamed of these facts, since both types of influence are directed to purposes that serve the interests of developing and industrial countries in achieving sound growth.

Anthony Looijen, Bank executive director representing both industrial and developing countries, cautioned against trying to turn all aid recipients into duplicates of the United States; it won't work. The World Bank must accept the political and economic systems that exist and provide a means through which member countries can benefit from the experience of other member countries and the Bank.

# Financing the Bank

MANFRED LAHNSTEIN

IN CONSIDERING IBRD and IDA financing we are faced with three questions: how should their activities be financed, up to what levels can they be financed, and what kind of activities should be financed?

There is a clear answer to the question of how IDA is to be financed: most of the money has to come from the budgets of Western industrial countries and from the capital surplus oil-exporting countries. It is less easy to say at what levels this should be done. There are two opposing forces at work: on the one hand, the heavy budgetary constraints of the industrial countries; and on the other hand, the desperate economic and financial position of the least developed countries, which are dependent on IDA credits as never before. Both forces cannot be fully satisfied at the same time. We have to find a delicate balance between them.

World Bank President Clausen said in his address to the annual meeting, "An IDA credit is not a welfare check. It is a productive investment." To my mind, this is a pertinent summing up. May it be fully accepted by governments and parliaments of all funding countries, the largest one included! IDA invests in the future of the least developed countries by furthering their economic and social progress. And it is a sound investment for the contributors. They, too, will benefit from promoting development in these countries, although benefits of this kind take time to materialize. They will never be achieved, however, unless IDA has sufficient resources to continue and expand its activities.

*Levels of IDA financing*

To take the difficult budget situation as the sole yardstick for determining the future level of IDA financing would be to put the realization of such benefits at grave risk. We should make it our goal to ensure that IDA remains dynamic in the long term. The IDA lending program must continue to grow, even if growth will have to be at more modest real rates than in the past.

There is a further important reason for ensuring the viability of IDA. It is not just one of many development aid institutions. It is one of the few institutions in which the industrial countries of the West can still exert decisive influence. IDA is, if you like, "our" institution. We should make it our common business to see to it that its characteristics are maintained. All industrial countries must take an equal interest and undertake absolutely reliable commitments. It is plainly unacceptable that a negotiated agreement to share the burden should be subsequently modified by a unilateral action. When this is done, as has happened in the case of the U.S. commitment, how can one expect other countries to step into the breach? On the contrary, one of the consequences would be a chain reaction to the detriment of all countries.

I urge our American friends to remedy the shortfall in meeting the U.S. commitment to IDA, which I personally consider to be deeply unsatisfactory. The U.S. image as a reliable partner is at stake. In the meantime, the consequences for IDA are clearly negative. Attempting to deal with this shortfall by increasing IBRD lending to the poorest countries would not constitute a satisfactory graduation policy. Furthermore, it would have consequences for the financing of the next general capital increase for the IBRD.

**Terms of IDA lending**

If we assume that the volume of IDA lending will in the future increase at a slower pace than before, we cannot escape the need to reflect on the recipients of IDA funds and, partially as an alternative to this, on changes in the terms of lending. I have two comments in this connection.

First, the present rate of lending to the least developed countries could be more or less maintained if IDA were to concentrate even more on those countries. This could be done, for instance, if some of the present borrowers were to gradually graduate out of the group of recipients of IDA resources. Another way would be to make the blend between IDA credits and World Bank loans harder in the case of countries that receive funds from both sources. However, there is not likely to be much scope for the redirection of IDA resources. IDA already concentrates its lending heavily on the least developed countries. What is more, these suggestions presuppose a corresponding capability on the part of the countries concerned to incur additional foreign debt on market terms. This would have to be carefully checked. Above all, a too hasty graduation could lead to a decline in the Bank's credit standing. Graduation should not be considered without all due precaution, whatever the pressures for it.

Second, a reconsideration of the terms of IDA lending is indeed called for. One might ask, for example, whether the fifty-year maturity is still appropriate. Other comparable institutions, such as the Asian Development Fund, make do with a forty-year maturity. It is also debatable whether lack of interest charges still makes sense. Perhaps IDA terms should be differentiated by borrower categories, to function for instance as a preparatory stage for later graduation. This would soften the shock effect of plunging into the cold water of normal World Bank loans. Some of these issues should certainly be tackled. However, while the flow of repayments would gradually increase as a result of changed lending conditions, this would not make enough difference to replace the donor country budgets as the main source of financing.

The World Bank, in comparison, obtains many times more than the paid-in proportion of its subscribed capital—which is all that affects the budget—by its own borrowings in the capital markets. These borrowings are the main source of finance for its lending operations.

*Expansion of lending*

A sharp increase in the Bank's lending operations was recently under discussion. The reasons are well known: lending for China, high inflation and interest rates, increased investment in the energy sector, and a growing demand for structural adjustment loans. It was decided (to my mind, correctly) that the existing capital basis of the World Bank would not permit so rapid an expansion of lending operations.

There are those who believe that the simplest way to permit a more rapid expansion in lending would be to alter the gearing ratio laid down in the Bank's statutes. However irresistible this idea may seem, it may turn out to be an oversimplification of the problem. While the gearing ratio does determine the level up to which the World Bank may have recourse to capital markets, it gives no indication of how much the Bank can actually borrow in these markets. The crucial factor in this respect is the soundness of the Bank's financial structure, and whether it is strong enough to support increasing borrowings. It would be of little use merely to alter the gearing ratio unless one could at the same time satisfy the market's requirements regarding the amount of callable capital, the earnings situation, and the liquidity position. In other words, altering the gearing ratio cannot obviate the need for a solid financial structure.

In any event, the subject of a change in the gearing ratio has to be approached with much caution. The share of total lending operations financed by borrowings has already increased rapidly. The adjustment of the interest rate charged on loans has not quite kept pace with this development. In the face of this situation, imposing extra credit charges or fees can be no more than a stopgap solution. I hope the recent decision to do this will be an exception, rather than a regular practice.

The effect of altering the gearing ratio and of dispensing with paid-in subscriptions in the case of a capital increase would be the same: the Bank would be forced to borrow even more. Moreover, the Bank's need to pass on the costs of its rapidly increasing borrowing to the recipients of its loans could ultimately make its terms insufficiently attractive to developing countries. In that event, the Bank would lose the capability to attain important development policy objectives. Both for this reason and to maintain a sound financial structure, the World Bank will continue to need sufficient capital, including a paid-in portion.

Let us be clear about one point: I have been talking about remedies which leave one part of the illness unaffected. The world is suffering from inflation and consequently from interest rates that are far too high, not only in the United States but in other industrialized countries and in the developing world.

The World Bank itself can probably do a great deal to determine the extent to which it will remain able to borrow the funds it needs in the market. There should be no insurmountable difficulties so long as the lending program does not appear to be exaggerated and the Bank concentrates on projects designed to achieve viable development policy objectives. Problems could arise, however, should the World Bank attempt to realize a loan volume that is no longer in conformity with these conditions and would have a detrimental effect on the Bank's own earnings situation.

In this context I would caution against the use of instruments such as borrowing at variable interest rates or indexation to protect principal repayments. Borrowing at variable interest rates does nothing to make the earnings situation of the World Bank easier to assess, and it creates uncertainty as to the cost burden imposed on developing countries. There are, finally, some strong arguments against the use of variable interest rates. This may appear to be a somewhat rigorous German point of view. But our resistance to variable interest rates has in our view contributed to the fact that our economy is still very responsive to interest rate movements and that the Bundesbank can effectively rely on this instrument in fighting inflation.

Whether or not the Bank should have extensive recourse to

private placements as a source of funds is a question that must b
answered on the strength of the prevailing market situation. Th
many uncertainties inherent in forecasts on the development c
the capital markets call for as flexible an approach as possible wit.
regard to diversification.

A welcome development would be the greater involvement c
the World Bank in the recycling of OPEC surpluses througl
direct borrowing in oil-exporting countries. As a consequence
we should accept a bigger financial and political role of thos
countries in World Bank matters, which could be a prelude to
debate we might have at the time of the next general capita
increase.

In addition, the World Bank should strive to make greater us
than it has to date of cofinancing, as this is one way of mobilizin;
more private capital for financing development projects.

## The Bank and the International Monetary Fund

The World Bank and the International Monetary Fund serve thei
members in a complementary, interrelated way. But their intendec
functions and responsibilities, as reflected in their charters, ar
clearly different.

The focus of the Bank is on supplying *long-term capital* in suppor
of specific development projects and programs. It stands ready tc
advise its members in working out sensible investment programs
establishing investment priorities, and evaluating projects.

The role of the Fund is to provide *temporary* balance of payment
finance while members adjust their economies. Normally it
policy advice should focus on macroeconomic variables relating
to monetary, fiscal, and exchange rate policies.

Through its "structural adjustment lending" introduced in 1980
the Bank has, in fact, established a facility for providing a forn
of assistance very similar to balance of payments finance. The
Fund, in turn, has recognized that the nature of the prevailing
economic imbalances may require longer adjustment periods anc
greater attention to the supply-side aspects of the world's economies. Thus, in today's world the line between the requirement;
of relatively short-term adjustment and those of long-term development has become more difficult to draw.

While the areas of interest common to the Bank and the Func
have widened, it is nevertheless essential to preserve their separate
and distinctive characteristics. It is a continuing challenge to botl
institutions to keep evolving flexibly in response to changing
needs of their members while not compromising their respective
fundamental objectives for which they were originally established.

A blurring of the functions of the Bank and the Fund could erode their financial support, weaken the confidence they enjoy in financial markets, and undermine the basis of their strength. Developing countries would be the first to suffer.

## Summary of Comments by Robert V. Roosa

THE POSSIBILITIES of increasing the role of the International Finance Corporation, the World Bank's affiliate chartered specifically to encourage the growth of private enterprise, deserve special attention.

The IFC's operations have grown rapidly in recent years, but its potential for mobilizing equity financing has barely been tapped. As countries move along the development spectrum, the IFC's role will become increasingly important, providing another means of expanding the leverage inherent in the World Bank system. Through equity participation, the IFC bestows a "Good Housekeeping seal of approval" on a private enterprise and at the same time furnishes a form of political risk insurance to investors, serving in both respects to attract private risk capital from domestic and foreign sources. Equity financing, moreover, has a special merit in light of the present and prospective debt-servicing problems of developing countries; unlike fixed interest and amortization obligations on debt capital, the repayment of equity capital can be postponed indefinitely, and the payment of dividends is dependent on the throw-off of earnings produced by the specific projects financed.

A number of possibilities for increasing the resources and role of the IFC are worth exploring. One possibility is additional direct borrowing from member governments. The IFC has one such placement outstanding, a $35 million loan from Saudi Arabia. The rest of its borrowing is from the World Bank itself. By trying more of such direct placements, the IFC could begin to equip itself to handle debt financing in its own name and on its own account. Altogether, the IFC's resources are comparatively small— approximately $1.2 billion, of which half consists of paid-in capital subscribed by the member governments and retained earnings and the rest of borrowing. The potential is there, however, to tap new sources of capital through direct borrowing activities.

A second possibility would be for the IFC to serve, in effect, as lead underwriter for the public marketing of securities issued by enterprises in developing countries. This would add a new dimension of third world access to world capital markets and would in effect be a simple extension of procedures alread employed by the IFC. That is, the IFC now participates as or equity holder among others in particular projects that are develope in part through the advice and guidance of its own engineerin and managerial staffs. The IFC also sells participations in existin loans or equity holdings, although the scale of such access t outside markets has thus far been relatively small. What it migl do now is to assist marginally creditworthy enterprises that me IFC standards in preparing market issues that could be offere either in the Eurocurrency market or in particular national capit markets. It could, in a sense, serve as managing underwriter fc the first market issues of such enterprises, relying on establishe channels for subsequent issues. Such offerings could be made i any of the currencies in which IBRD lending now takes plac and could possibly be for maturities in the five-year range c longer.

Third, the IFC might begin to offer its own obligations on th public market. The time may not yet be at hand, but at som point the IFC's credit position and requirements, including i ability to make use of variable-rate arrangements, might b sufficiently differentiated from that of the Bank as to make separat public debt offerings worthwhile. If so, such offerings would ad to the potential resources available to the system as a whole.

A fourth source of funds would be an increase in the capital c the IFC. The last increase in paid-in capital—from $150 millio to $450 million—took place in 1977. An increase of the same scal some time within the next few years would provide a larger bas for an expansion in IFC's equity financing and for new forms c IFC borrowing.

Earlier in the meeting George Shultz called for new initiativ and creativity to meet the Bank's needs in the 1980s. The IF( offers this kind of potential.

## Summary of Comments by James D. Wolfensohn

THE PERCEPTION of the World Bank in Europe, the United States and Japan, based on very recent soundings, continues to be on of a healthy international borrower. To date it has borrowed one third of its requirements in U.S. dollars and two-thirds in othe currencies. It is welcome in all the major capital markets and it prospects look good.

At the same time, it must be recognized that the World Bank like all industrial borrowers, must operate within a turbulent an difficult market. For the Bank, moreover, additional complications arise because of the internal issues—for example, U.S. difficulties in obtaining appropriations for IDA—to which Lahnstein referred.

The problem of operating in today's markets cannot be over-stressed. Interest rates and exchange rates have never been so volatile. Concern exists about the quality of banks, savings institutions, and other borrowers. In this environment, the prospects of all borrowers are under review; the World Bank is not exempt from this reassessment. While it has social responsibilities, it is judged in the market as a financial entity with its own parameters of borrowing limitations, earnings, and lending policies.

In the U.S. market, there is some evidence of a change in perception of the Bank as a quality instrument for investment. This is reflected in the spread between the most recent Bank issues and benchmark Treasury issues of 130 basis points for the five-year maturity and 160 basis points for the ten-year maturity; such large spreads are unprecedented for the Bank. A similar widening of spreads applies now to other borrowers, industrial companies and foreign governments alike. Nonetheless, the fact remains that the cost of borrowing by the World Bank has substantially increased.

In this difficult environment, the Bank faces gross borrowing requirements of some $50 billion and net borrowing requirements of $25 billion to $30 billion over the next five years. This is a substantial amount to borrow when private markets are not as open as they once were and the investment community, although positive in its attitude toward the Bank, is nonetheless generally apprehensive. Management will continue to face difficult questions of judgment as to when and how it should enter markets to seek financing.

Another complicating factor is the current interest rate gap on the $28 billion in undisbursed commitments. The average lending rate on these commitments is 8.6 percent, while the current average borrowing cost is 11 percent. This gap could be met by a capital increase sometime in the mid-1980s, which would involve a paid-in portion. It would not be helped at all by an increase in lending authority deriving from a change in the gearing ratio. Nor will the new 1.5 percent front-end fee be enough.

This interest rate gap will have to be faced in one way or another, or the problem could compound over the future. This raises the question of whether the Bank should go to floating interest rates—for funding alone, for lending, or for both.

Finally, it is well to remember that large borrowers—the international banks—have access to a lender of last resort in the Federal Reserve, the Bank of England, and central banks elsewhere. This gives confidence to those who lend to these institutions. The World Bank, on the other hand, is dependent on expressions of support by member governments and by the statements and assessments of financial experts who know something about the quality and standing of the institution. In this connection, the continuing debate in the United States about the merits of appropriating funds for IDA or for the capital increase are not helpful. The fragile investment community must be nurtured. The private sector is not obliged to invest in the World Bank; it needs expressions of support and confidence to continue doing so.

## General Discussion

GARCIA-PARRA congratulated Lahnstein for highlighting the distinction between IDA and the Bank. IDA credits are highly concessional because they are provided only to the poorest countries, which generally are not yet creditworthy; Bank loans are on commercial terms, taking into account the exchange risk the borrower must bear. In fact, a capital infusion may be necessary to prevent the Bank from pricing itself out of the market. Industrial countries should understand that capital subscriptions to the Bank are not aid but a productive investment that pays much higher commercial rates of return to them, as measured by the resulting increase in exports, than comparable investments in export-financing institutions such as the Export-Import Bank. The World Bank has proven to be effective and successful; in view of the worsening world economic outlook, it will have to play an even larger role in the future.

Nicholas Rey of Merrill Lynch pointed out that cofinancing could be an additional source of capital, but care should be exercised that it does not simply replace normal lending by commercial banks. This danger is greatest in the newly industrializing countries, which already have ready access to commercial bank financing. The Bank should put more emphasis, therefore, on cofinancing in those developing countries that are not yet experienced or well-known borrowers in private markets. Another possibility is to attract institutional funds (insurance companies and pension funds) to cofinance Bank projects. This would be an additional source of capital, but it would require that the Bank provide greater surety to such investors, either through the subordination of its own share of the loan or through stronger cross-default clauses.

Vance Van Dine of Morgan Stanley said that too much should not be drawn from an increase in the spread between Treasury and World Bank issues at any given time. These spreads always change—widely in today's market. Since the last World Bank issue in the United States, to which Wolfensohn referred, the spread has narrowed substantially. It is true that the investment community is taking a hard look at the credit of the Bank, but it is unfair to draw inferences from that, one way or the other.

A participant said the Bank was losing the means of carrying out its objectives. Lending requirements were growing because of China's membership, structural adjustment loans, and energy investment requirements. At the same time, resources were more limited and costly. If funds in the industrial countries were being closed off, the Bank should do more to borrow from capital surplus oil-exporting countries, as Lahnstein had suggested. As to costs, variable lending rates would not help and could be harmful.

Lahnstein said that the confidence factor in the Bank's capital situation, to which Wolfensohn referred, should be taken into account when discussions begin on the next capital increase for the Bank. The confidence problem was also part of the background he had in mind when he urged the United States to meet its financial commitments to IDA; performance in meeting this commitment could affect the level of confidence about whether U.S. political commitments will be met in other areas.

Roosa added that financing difficulties are complicated by the variability of exchange rates. To tap available funds, the Bank markets issue in various currencies, which adds exchange risks to the costs the borrower must bear. To make the interest rates also variable may overload the circuit.

Hartley said since funds are scarce, it is all the more important to leave the energy sector to private industry. Lead times in energy projects are long, capital requirements large, and risks substantial. In these circumstances, equity financing is all the more helpful.

Wolfensohn said that the image and reputation of the Bank in financial markets is still first class; the increase in the spread mentioned in his earlier remarks does not alter that image. In fact, yields on Bank issues are the equivalent of those now applying to outstanding issues of the governments of Germany and Japan. The point to be stressed is that the volatility of the U.S. market has created new problems for the World Bank, as it has for other borrowers.

A participant said that hardening the blend between IDA credits and Bank loans, as Lahnstein suggested, would penalize countries that had managed their affairs prudently. Would not poor countries be sacrificed for still poorer countries?

Lahnstein acknowledged the point and said this should be avoided if possible. However there are risks and penalties in not considering these kinds of changes.

Leonard Silk of the *New York Times* argued that the confidence problem has been raised as a factor affecting the Bank's financial position. What is the true attitude of the U.S. administration toward the Bank? Deputy Secretary MacNamar said the administration strongly supports the Bank. On the other hand, U.S. appropriations for the Bank are lagging, and even at this late date the administration has failed to appoint a U.S. executive director. Furthermore, ideological talk from sources within the administration implies that foreign aid is bad and the Bank is just another foreign aid agency. A second point is the volatility of interest and exchange rates, which adversely affect the operations of the Bank. It has been charged, by the German chancellor and the German economic minister among others, that U.S. policy is partly at fault.

Charls Walker, former deputy secretary of the treasury, replied that a U.S. executive director was named but tragically died before he could take office.

To repeat what Deputy Secretary MacNamar said, the best contribution this country can make to the future success and sustainability of the World Bank is to restore noninflationary growth to this country. We are now in a transitional stage where there is a wide difference of opinion as to whether the country is on course. He is pleased about the accomplishment of a declining inflation rate, which has not received the attention it deserves, and a probably significant increase in the savings rate, resulting from increased confidence, the tax cut, and the new incentive provided by individual retirement accounts. The influence of a declining inflation rate on the shift from real to financial assets also bodes well. U.S. domestic policies are on track and that is the best contribution we can make to the Bank.

Barr said he had supported the work of the World Bank over the past twenty-three years and feels that it has been the best investment of time and energy he has made. He hopes the administration understands the reasons for this point of view.

# A Concluding Perspective

A. W. CLAUSEN

TODAY'S conference has been exactly what a good discussion on a critical set of questions ought to be: thoughtful, candid, straightforward, and with no holds barred. Let me take in turn each of the topics of the four discussion panels and add some brief observations.

I think that you know pretty well where I stand. After all, the private sector is what I know best and what I have called home for more than thirty-one years. As a commercial banker, my whole career was spent in that competitive, creative, energetic marketplace. I have to say honestly that I loved it, and I still do.

So when anyone in the international community mounts the rostrum and says firmly that the private sector ought to be more involved in the development effort, I am always the first one in the congregation to say: "Amen!" I know it works. What is more, most of our developing member countries know it works too.

*The private sector*

The private sector, after all, currently generates well over half of the gross domestic product of the developing world. There are broad sectors in many of those economies where private enterprise can be an immensely effective agent for furthering economic development.

It is true, as has been mentioned, that the World Bank does not try to tell any member country what kind of political ideology it ought to have. That is because we are not in the ideology business. So critics who say that the World Bank policies help promote socialism are as off the mark as those who say its policies help promote laissez-faire capitalism. "Isms" are just not in our inventory. They are not our mandate. But pragmatic economic progress is.

That is why the Bank can and does work successfully with countries from all points on the ideological compass, provided only that they are willing to be realistic and careful not to substitute doctrine for data, or philosophy for facts.

The World Bank's basic objective is precisely the same in any

of our developing member countries: to assist the country both
to accelerate its economic growth and enhance the economic
opportunities of its people, and thus make possible a better standard
of living for all. But while we in the Bank do not climb into the
pulpit and preach what kind of a political creed a country ought
to espouse, we are not bashful about pointing out what the world's
economic experience demonstrates.

In the post–World War II period, that experience is very clear.
Those countries that have demonstrated the best economic performance have encouraged their private sectors. That is not
surprising because it means that they have simply encouraged a
human characteristic that is universal, though unfortunately still
latent in some societies: the entrepreneurial energy inherent in
their own citizenry.

Now, of course, the Bank's own affiliate, the International
Finance Corporation, has the specific catalytic role to help put
joint investment packages together in order to fund private
enterprise ventures in our developing member countries—ventures
without government guarantees, but with a high development
component.

The IFC has been doing this successfully now for a quarter of
a century. So successfully, in fact, that in terms of dollar volume,
the IFC's board in fiscal year 1981 alone approved investments
equal to the total approved in the first fifteen years of the
corporation's history.

But it is not just the IFC that is involved with the private
sector. About half of all World Bank lending is also directed to
activities in that sector. One of the principal messages of the
Bank's recent report on sub-Saharan Africa, for example, is that
the economic growth in the countries in this area can be accelerated
by the more effective use of their domestic private sectors and by
creating a policy framework that is more supportive for development. As the domestic private sector grows in a developing
country, so too the environment for more foreign private equity
investment ought to improve.

The IBRD is also very much at home with the private sector
through its cofinancing program with the private banking community. The number of operations providing for cofinancing with
commercial banks has burgeoned from an average of ten a year
in the 1977–79 fiscal year period to twenty a year in fiscal years
1980–81. In the same period volume expanded from $400 million
a year to $1.7 billion a year.

Altogether, 187 banks worldwide have cooperated with us in

cofinancing. Thirty-six of these have been U.S. banks. They have provided about 24 percent of the funding in deals already arranged. The Japanese banks have provided 22 percent, and the United Kingdom and European banks about 33 percent.

We want very much to expand such cofinancing, and to accomplish that we need to do three things: to provide more information on countries and projects to potential cofinancing partners on a timely basis; to diversify the means by which we can jointly finance these projects in creditworthy countries; and, finally, to involve a much larger number of banks. We are working on all three of these fronts.

And just last month senior officers representing more than twenty-five U.S. banks met with us here in Washington for a full day's seminar on cofinancing. We plan to do much more of this kind of basic briefing: explaining the advantages of having the World Bank as a partner, pointing out the investment opportunities, and outlining the unique services that the World Bank can provide in helping private banks to arrive at sound lending decisions in development projects. In our fiscal year 1982–83 pipeline, there are over 100 projects suitable, we think, for commercial bank cofinancing.

But beyond cofinancing, there still are other potential areas in which the World Bank can, and I believe should, act as a catalyst in bringing more of the private sector into the international development scene. One is the creation of a practical multilateral insurance agency.

The principal reason that the private sector in the developed nations does not invest more readily in the developing countries is neither because these entrepreneurs are indifferent to the fate of the developing world, nor because they feel there are no attractive projects.

It is rather because they are understandably uneasy over the absence of reasonable security against certain kinds of political risks that cannot always be met by the authorities of the developing country alone, or by the individual national insurance plans that a number of developed countries have already initiated.

There is some renewed interest in a multilateral investment insurance agency that would complement the activities of the national agencies now in existence. As I have indicated, we in the Bank are prepared to assist in the effort to explore the feasibility of establishing such a mechanism.

The second area is a growing need for a general set of agreements on the whole issue of international investment. If international investment is going to be the effective driving force of development that it can become in the 1980s and beyond, then it has to reflect the essential interest of all the parties involved.

These interests do overlap at certain points. What a general agreement on international investment could achieve is to identify these points of common interest and try to widen and bolster them to the benefit of all the parties involved.

What we need specifically is an international framework that could provide the machinery for negotiating away the narrowly nationalistic policies that discourage international investment. We have achieved that up to a point in the field of international trade. That system today is far from perfect, but it has made very real progress against shortsighted and self-defeating barriers to trade. And it does have a framework in place for ongoing negotiations to make things work better. But in international investment policy, no such broad global framework yet exists.

I believe we need one. And I am grateful that George Shultz, Bob Hormats at the State Department, Fred Bergsten, and others are taking up the cudgel in raising our awareness of this issue and this need. I think the time may be right to start examining this matter seriously. Certainly the Bank is ready to join in such an exploratory effort.

*Energy investments*

As I indicated at our recent annual meeting, energy definitely is going to be a priority sector for the Bank in the 1980s. The reason is obvious: adequate supplies of energy are absolutely essential for progress in any developing society. And that, in turn, means that a primary objective in the oil-importing developing countries will be to increase their own domestic production of energy.

In 1980 the Bank submitted to its board for consideration an expanded program of energy lending in its developing member countries which amounted to $25 billion, covering the fiscal years 1981 through 1985. About half the program was in electric power; one-third was in gas and oil development; and the remainder was in such areas as fuel wood, coal, conservation, and biomass development.

The Bank believed that roughly half the expanded energy lending could be financed from its own resources, and that some additional and separate method of financing would be required for the rest. The precise form that financing should take has not yet been agreed upon.

In the absence of such an agreement, we plan this fiscal year to lend some $3 billion for all types of energy projects. This represents a 25 percent increase over the $2.3 billion we lent last year, and it will boost the share of our lending for the energy sector to almost a quarter of our total lending for everything.

It is clear that the Bank takes the energy problem seriously. But in my view, far too much attention has been focused on the lack of agreement over the precise means of financing additional World Bank lending for energy, and not nearly enough attention on the importance and value to everyone in the international community of the expanded lending program itself.

The fact is that the program can add substantially to the availability of locally produced oil, gas, and coal in the developing countries, and, together with the development of domestic hydro-resources and conservation measures, will permit further reduction in these countries' dependence on imported oil.

Now, the need for that today is no less than it was in 1980. If anything, the urgency of the problem is even greater. For many of our developing member countries, the high cost of imported energy continues to be a major burden on their balance of payments, and absorbs in some cases as much as 90 percent of their export earnings.

So the basic objective of the Bank in all of this is to find additional funds for a more adequate energy lending program for those developing member countries that badly need it. And our primary concern clearly is not to insist on one specific means of accomplishing that rather than another.

The idea of a World Bank energy affiliate has merit, particularly because it would have the flexibility of having a separate corporate entity—with a voting structure that could vary from that of the IBRD or IDA. And yet it would not have the costly disadvantage of having to create an additional bureaucracy, or be burdened with the tendency to overspecialize and separate energy-sector problems from overall integrated development planning.

But if the time or circumstances are not ripe for such an affiliate, then there are alternative approaches. One would be to establish bilateral lines of credit from as many countries as wish to participate to help finance the Bank's expanded energy lending program. The estimated amount of priority energy projects which we could not finance directly from the Bank's resources rises from about $1 billion in fiscal year 1982 to $2 billion in fiscal year 1983 and to a little under $4 billion in fiscal year 1984.

Even if a small group of donor countries were willing to assure the Bank of the availability of cofinancing for energy projects on a reasonably automatic basis, we would be prepared to incur the staff costs necessary to develop the projects for financing. And inasmuch as we have already assumed substantial cofinancing in our forward planning, it is clear that the establishment of such a facility would require either additional resources to be made available by the participating countries, or a shift in their sectoral aid priorities.

Another approach would be the creation of a trust fund to be administered by the Bank. Contributions would be voluntary, although their volume, of course, would have to be significant, and the conditions of financing compatible with our operating procedures.

Still another approach would be for countries to agree in advance to purchase for their own account portions of bank loans or IDA credits made for energy projects. This would replenish our resources, and if sufficient countries participated we could afford to incur the cost of staff expansion to prepare the additional volume of projects for lending.

Yet another approach would be to expand the Bank's lending program for energy over and beyond presently planned levels now that the Bank's shareholders have authorized its general capital increase.

All, or most, of the capital increase could be earmarked for energy development. Thus far our member countries, including our major shareholders, have been reluctant to consider such an expansion, but it could be done without any budgetary consequences to them.

Such additional Bank lending, if not in the full amount required to meet the additional investments in energy, could of course be associated with one or another of these alternate approaches.

But I want to repeat: what is of the first importance in this particular issue is not the details of the approach, but rather the consensus on the nature of the energy problem in the developing countries and the resolve to find substantive solutions.

We in the Bank remain convinced that the expansion of lending for energy in our developing member countries is crucial, and that some of this lending has to be financed with additional resources.

We are equally convinced that if this critical support for energy development in these hard-pressed societies is to be of assistance in time to avoid substantial damage to their overall development, then existing institutions have to be utilized and new bureaucracies and management structures have to be avoided.

*Multilateral and bilateral aid*

The respective roles of multilateral and bilateral aid never really need be a problem. The plain truth of the matter is that both multilateral and bilateral assistance are indispensable—not only for the developing countries themselves, but for the donor countries as well.

Of course, donor nations are going to try to further their foreign policy objectives through bilateral aid programs. That is normal and inevitable. But the case for multilateral programs in an interdependent world in which development goes far beyond short-term and shifting political alliances is just as critical.

Both forms of development assistance—provided they are hardheaded and sensible—are very much in everyone's interest. What is called for is reasonable cooperation and coordination in making all these various programs mesh together and work. In that matter, the Bank can be exceptionally useful precisely because it has no political affiliation or ideological commitment. That makes it possible for the Bank to play a fair and rigorously rational role in the coordination process, and to concern itself exclusively with pragmatic economics.

The Bank, of course, has had immense experience in coordinating development assistance. We currently are chairing twenty-one active consortia and consultative groups for precisely that purpose. But while it has become the world's largest international development institution, the Bank clearly cannot do everything that needs to be done in the development field, and certainly should not try to.

But if all the major elements at work in this international endeavor—multilateral, bilateral, the private sector, and various specialized groups—could be linked into closer and more effective cooperation, then the possibilities for greater progress could be substantially improved.

One very obvious matter in which greater cooperation is desirable is in the donor countries' allocation of their official development assistance between the poorest developing societies—which of course need it the most—and the middle- and high-income developing countries, which are substantially better off.

Given the fact that flows of concessional capital—which is what development assistance is by definition—have largely stagnated as a percentage of donor GNP over the decade of the 1970s, it is particularly depressing to reflect that the portion allocated to the poorest countries is so small in both relative and absolute amounts. The blunt fact is that on a per capita basis, the low-income countries receive less concessional assistance today than do the middle-income developing nations. That does not make good sense, and that is an area in which multilateral institutions and bilateral agencies ought to be able to work more closely together.

*Financing the*
*Bank*

I have already touched on bank financing as it relates to our expanded energy program, but let me say a word or two on the overall IDA and IBRD outlook.

We are all aware that IDA's sixth replenishment has had a rough time in Congress. And we all know that the final outcome was that Congress appropriated $700 million for fiscal year 1982.

What we ought not to forget is that IDA got that $700 million from Congress—rather than a lot less—only because many members of the House and Senate, and the administration, worked very hard to make it happen. We in the Bank are deeply grateful for those efforts. It has been a very difficult process all around for everyone concerned.

Now we are faced with another difficult set of choices. It is clear that we are not going to have sufficient IDA funding to meet our planned operational targets.

As you know, other donor countries may prorate their IDA contributions in line with the U.S. total. Even if some members contribute more than that, we estimate that we will have only about $2.6 billion in IDA resources available to us in fiscal year 1982 instead of the planned $4.1 billion. That means that we have to retool our plans as carefully as we can and look for instances in which we can provide more IBRD loans in order to offset to some degree the cuts we will have to make in our planned IDA commitments. In some IDA countries we may be able to introduce some initial blending of IDA and IBRD funds; and in others, in which we already are blending, we will have to harden the mix.

The opening discussions for the seventh replenishment are scheduled to get under way this year. No one pretends that they are going to be very easy. We are in an era of budgetary restraints in most of the donor countries. While there is absolutely no question that IDA has been an immensely successful and worthwhile investment over the past twenty years, the political will to make adequate concessional development assistance available to the poorest developing countries is losing ground in some quarters.

IDA itself was, of course, originally largely an American idea. It was launched in a conservative Republican administration in 1960, and its purpose was in part to broaden burden sharing among OECD countries in order to make official development assistance available in the developing countries that needed help desperately, but were simply not creditworthy for funds on market or even IBRD terms.

The success of IDA is that it did precisely what it set out to do. It did broaden the burden sharing among the donor countries, and it did assist many countries to graduate from low-income to middle-income economies. Among them were Korea, the Philippines, Thailand, the Ivory Coast, and some fifteen similar cases. Today those countries are vigorous and valuable trading partners with the developed nations. IDA clearly has turned out to be a wise and effective investment.

In the meantime, the United States—whose official development assistance in 1949, at the beginning of the Marshall Plan, amounted to 2.79 percent of its GNP, and was 2.53 percent in 1960, the year IDA was founded—now devotes only about 0.25 percent of its GNP to official development assistance. This is far below the OECD's Development Assistance Committee member-country average of 0.37 percent, and is, in fact, the lowest percentage of any major industrial OECD country, save Italy.

And the U.S. share of the burden in IDA has diminished from 41 percent at the inception of IDA in 1960 to 27 percent in IDA VI, the current replenishment. IDA, however, remains the world's most important single source of concessional assistance for the poorest of the poor developing countries, and I do not believe that the United States will turn its back on those hundreds of millions of individuals who only want a chance to improve their own economic performance.

But the transfer of resources that has been referred to is not really the issue here. IDA is not the International Red Cross, or a global soup kitchen, or even a row of cheery Christmas stockings hung cozily on the world's hearth. And while the symbolism for IDA may not be Ebenezer Scrooge, it clearly is not Santa Claus either.

The right way to think about IDA is to think of it for what it actually is: an international investment and development institution, owned and operated by the world's governments, and founded specifically to serve its poorest developing member countries, which cannot yet afford to borrow on IBRD or market terms. In every other respect, save the terms, IDA has the same rigorous standards as the IBRD. There simply is no difference at all in the project quality or priority.

I have spent my working life in the world of investment, and I know what sound, high-priority, carefully managed investments can do to transform an economy. There are many low-income economies in the developing world today that can transform themselves faster than either they or others may think possible. That has happened many times in the past twenty years, confounding everyone's expectations. It is going to continue to happen over the next twenty years. But that takes investment—mostly, of course, domestic investment, but some external investment as well.

As I have pointed out recently, if IDA were just a kind of international entitlement program—just a relic of a more prosperous economic period in the past when the United States felt more generous—then I could understand that in a time of budgetary pressures it might make good economic sense to cut it back, and pare it down, and string it out in a severely reduced form.

But IDA is not an international entitlement program. And the basic issue is not generosity. On the contrary, IDA is a hardheaded investment in international trade, economic growth, and greater global stability and cohesion.

The United States ought to live up to the international agreements it has made with respect to IDA because it is in its own best self-interest to do so. That is true of every donor country that contributes to IDA, and there are thirty-three countries that do.

But all of this is not to say that IDA ought to be inflexible, or that the mechanism of replenishment cannot be improved, or that every detail that was laid down in 1960 when IDA first came into being is now set firmly in concrete. Flexibility and openness to sensible change is, after all, the indispensable ingredient required in any living, growing, organic institution that wants to succeed in an evolutionary environment. Not changes of principle, mind you, but changes of procedure and practice.

The IDA credit—considered simply as a product design of the World Bank—is now twenty years old. Its terms essentially have remained unchanged: a fifty-year maturity; ten years of grace; no interest charge; and a three-quarters of 1 percent service charge on disbursed balances.

Just this past Tuesday, our board made the first slight alteration in IDA terms since its inception. On future IDA credits, in addition to the traditional three-quarters of 1 percent service charge on the disbursed balances, there will be a new one-half of 1 percent service charge on the undisbursed balances.

This change was made to rectify what has become a basic

asymmetry in IDA's income. Its main administration expenses arise at the beginning and at an early stage, during project preparation and start-up activities. But the income from the traditional service charge does not start flowing until much later, when the credit is being gradually disbursed as the project proceeds.

This timing mismatch between cost and repayment has entailed operating deficits to IDA since 1976. These deficits were covered at first by using up accumulated surpluses from earlier years. Since more deficits of this type were expected in future years, the time had come to correct the mismatch. The newly approved service charge on undisbursed balances will enable IDA to recover its costs more promptly, without making its credits significantly more costly.

This is a small and beneficial change. Other changes—not as small, but perhaps even more beneficial—are worth at least exploring. And when I say "beneficial" here, I mean to the entire membership of IDA: to the donors and recipients alike, as well as to the association itself.

The original IDA formula calls for credits to be extended to IDA recipients at zero percent interest for fifty years. If the individual IDA recipient countries are doing their job well and making better than average development progress, and if the World Bank is doing its job well and continues to help these countries through further IDA credits and then IBRD loans, and economic advice and technical assistance flows throughout, then, theoretically at least, there ought to come a time ultimately when increases in new replenishment grants to IDA from donor countries could slow down.

They could slow down because the volume of repayments received by IDA from credit extensions, using earlier replenishments, will start to become significant. And these repayments can be used in perpetuity for recycling over and over and over again.

But that point in time, under the existing IDA product design, takes a very, very long time indeed. Even by the end of this decade, eight years from now when IDA will be celebrating its thirtieth birthday, the annual aggregate of repayments from IDA credits extended during the decades of the 1960s and 1970s will approximate only $200 million a year.

IDA money is out there now for fifty years and a great deal can happen in fifty years. There can be a lot of successes that no one anywhere can anticipate ten, twenty, or twenty-five years before. That really is exactly what has been happening. Look at Korea and the Philippines and some twenty-two other countries, including Chile, Turkey, Jordan, the Ivory Coast, and Colombia. They have graduated from IDA.

This phenomenon and experience raises the question as to whether we ought to start thinking of IDA more in terms of its recycling potential. At least theoretically there ought to be a way to design an equitable trigger mechanism in future IDA credits—that is, credits that are not yet negotiated—which would provide for countries that have been IDA graduates for some years to accelerate the repayment of their IDA balances after they have reached a certain level of development progress on a comparative basis.

The same kind of equitable trigger mechanism could perhaps be designed and put in place in the future IBRD loans as well, which now typically have twenty-year maturities. Countries having reached a certain level of progress, or having graduated from the IBRD, might then accelerate their repayments of outstanding balances so that these funds, too, could be recycled more quickly into new loans for other countries that have not been as successful in their economic development progress.

As I say, these at the moment are merely speculations. But I think they are worth exploring because, as matters stand, both IDA and the IBRD are very limited as recycling instrumentalities. They have the potential, at least, of becoming more effective recycling mechanisms.

Now, let me say a few more words specifically about the IBRD. Overall, our total borrowing volume this year may exceed $8 billion. It may be over $9 billion next year and $10 billion a year later. To support these plans we are having productive discussions with our underwriters here and with key institutions abroad.

The board also recently approved the introduction of a front-end fee of 1.5 percent on the face value of all new IBRD loans. The borrower can either pay this fee from its own resources when the loan is approved, or capitalize it by adding the one-time charge itself to the loan. This action was taken to forestall any potential decline in the Bank's income over the medium term as a result of adverse movements in exchange rates and interest rates. It will generate more revenues promptly and will strengthen the Bank's standing in the international capital markets.

I think it is important to emphasize two points here. First, Bank financing is not concessional. IBRD lending is not a "taxpayers' handout," as has been suggested. Our loan interest charges (currently 11.6 percent per annum) are based on cost—plus a modest markup—but there is a lagged timing mismatch.

Notwithstanding that phenomenon (which I will explain in a moment), we do earn a return on our paid-in capital of about 8 percent.

IDA, however, is different. Here there is no interest charge on the credits extended, but only a modest service charge designed to cover its costs. But remember, IDA uses grant money received from donor countries, and not borrowed money from the marketplace.

The second point I would make is this. The IBRD needs to be careful about the level of its net income and the general trend of its profitability over a period of years because it is *not* dependent on taxpayers' money as a source of its funds. It is reliant, rather, on the international marketplace as a source of most of its funds, and therefore it needs to be able to maintain a strong financial position to be able to access the capital markets at the finest rates possible.

But now that the Bank has established a front-end fee to help stabilize its income, a much wider task needs to be addressed. We need to improve the Bank's overall financial flexibility and examine ways to reduce its exposure to unnecessary interest rate risks.

There is, in the current financial environment, a stubborn structural problem. It is the problem of having committed loans to be disbursed in future years at fixed interest rates—rates fixed at one point in time—and then subsequently funding those commitments in later periods when the financial markets are in a much different (and, in recent years, a much more difficult and volatile) environment than that existing at the time the loans were committed.

Additionally, there has been a gradual and growing reluctance on the part of investors to purchase long-term bonds at fixed rates because of the trends of ever-higher interest rates over at least the last fifteen years or so, and because of the inflationary expectations for the future years.

These realities of the marketplace require that we be increasingly and aggressively innovative in meeting our borrowing requirements with the use of swap arrangements, indexed currency borrowings, and floating-rate securities, where appropriate. The wide swings in market rates over the years, and the volatility existing in the international markets generally, are forcing us to at least consider whether we should introduce a degree of variability in our lending rates, as well as whether we should tap the more plentiful short-term markets at the appropriate times and in appropriate amounts.

At the same time, we recognize that the World Bank is first, last, and always a development bank and that we should avoid even the appearance of a commercial bank in our approach to lending. Nevertheless, how the burden of interest rate risk can be moderated or shared or avoided in future years is a basic financial issue which we are constantly addressing and shall continue to do so in order to maintain the superb financial condition that currently exists.

In the meantime, of course, the agreement on our general capital increase has now come into effect, and it is important that our member countries move forward with their subscriptions. When these are completed they will boost the IBRD's capital from about $42 billion to more than $82 billion at current exchange rates.

My view is that we should look for further lending capacity in the IBRD in future years through the mechanism of additional general capital increases, and not through a change in the gearing ratio. New capital subscriptions are cheap, in budgetary terms, for our member countries, and indeed can theoretically be without any cost whatsoever if the paid-in portion is reduced to zero.

I am not recommending that, but there is little risk involved in additional capital subscriptions since any calls on this capital in the future are extremely remote and highly unlikely, given the sound lending practices of the Bank; an enviable experience, unmatched anywhere else, of never having suffered a default in its thirty-six-year existence; and, moreover, a policy, without exception, of never refinancing any of the obligations owed to it. It should be emphasized that calls on capital can only be made for the purpose of paying off its borrowed indebtedness.

What I believe finally emerges out of all that we have discussed is an image of the World Bank as a unique institution. And that it is. It is not unique because it has problems. Every institution has problems. It is not unique because it is controversial. Every institution that tries to do something important is controversial. And, finally, it is not unique because it is complex and diverse. Complexity and diversity have become commonplace today.

The World Bank is unique, I think, because it is, in fact, a prototype institution for our particular era of history. And what characterizes our era? Interdependence. Noisy, argumentative, complicated, but ultimately inescapable, interdependence.

The plain truth is that the world of investment and development, like the world of almost everything else today, has become much more interdependent than many of us realize. Even those of us who like to use the word *interdependence*—and most of us do—

still have difficulty in trying to grasp the pace of this change in underlying international relationships today. The result is that one of our basic problems is simply trying to adjust and update our thinking in order to get it into some kind of a reasonable sync with the rush of reality.

The fact of interdependence today is far in advance of its public perception. That is why government and institutions and individuals have difficulty in designing policies today that reflect fully their own national best interests.

The World Bank—thanks to the men of vision who designed it toward the close of the most devastating conflict in history, in July 1944—will, I think, be regarded one day as a prototype institution for the opening decades of the era of international interdependence. The Bank works, and works well, because it is owned by 141 member countries, diverse in every respect save this: they agree that development is a global job that must add up to a plus-sum game, a game in which everyone can win and no one need lose.

# Conference Participants

Willis W. Alexander
*Executive Vice-President, American Bankers Association*

J. W. Anderson
*Editorial Writer, The Washington Post*

John Anson
*World Bank Executive Director for the United Kingdom*

Robert L. Ayres
*Senior Fellow, Overseas Development Council*

Frank C. Ballance
*President, Action for World Development*

Nicolas Ardito-Barletta
*World Bank Vice-President, Latin America and the Caribbean*

Joseph W. Barr
*Corporate Director and Former Secretary of the Treasury*

Adrian A. Basora
*Director, Office of Development Finance, Department of State*

Munir P. Benjenk
*World Bank Vice-President, External Relations*

C. Fred Bergsten
*Director, Institute for International Economics*

John Bolton
*General Counsel, U.S. International Development Cooperation Agency*
*Agency for International Development*

Henry Brandon
*Chief American Correspondent and Associate Editor, London Sunday Times*

Alexander Brummer
*Washington Correspondent, Guardian of London*

Thomas Buergenthal
*Dean, Washington College of Law, The American University*

Samuel E. Bunker
*Administrator, International Programs Division*
*National Rural Electric Cooperative Association*

John R. Bunten
*Vice-Chairman, RepublicBank Dallas*

Vincent C. Burke, Jr.
*Chairman of the Board, The Riggs National Bank*

83

James T. Byrne, Jr.
*Vice-President and Director, Public Affairs, Bankers Trust Company*

Carol Capps
*Chair, International Development Assistance Policy Work Group*
*Interreligious Task Force on U.S. Food Policy*

William D. Carmichael
*Vice-President, Developing Country Programs, The Ford Foundation*

Edward W. Carter
*Chairman of the Board, Carter Hawley Hale Stores, Inc.*

Hui Chen
*World Bank Alternate Executive Director for China*

Warren M. Christopher
*Chairman and Senior Partner, O'Melveny and Myers*
*Former Deputy Secretary of State*

George J. Clark
*Executive Vice-President, Citibank, N.A.*

A. W. Clausen
*President, The World Bank*

Elinor G. Constable
*Deputy Assistant Secretary for International Finance and Development*
*Department of State*

Edward Cowan
*Correspondent, The New York Times*

Neil H. Cullen
*Director of Administration, The Brookings Institution*

Thomas C. Dawson
*Deputy Assistant Secretary (Developing Nations)*
*Department of the Treasury*

Edwin A. Deagle, Jr.
*Director, International Relations, The Rockefeller Foundation*

Jacques de Groote
*World Bank Executive Director for Austria, Belgium, Luxembourg, and Turkey*

J. de Larosière
*Managing Director and Chairman of the Executive Board*
*International Monetary Fund*

Bruno de Maulde
*World Bank Executive Director for France*

William A. Delphos
*Vice-President for Operations*
*Overseas Private Investment Corporation*

Alvin Drischler
*Deputy Assistant Secretary of State for Congressional Relations*
*Department of State*

Joy Dunkerley
*Senior Fellow, Resources for the Future*

Elise R. W. du Pont
*Assistant Administrator, Bureau for Private Enterprise*
*Agency for International Development*

Philip A. DuSault
*Deputy Associate Director for International Affairs*
*Office of Management and Budget*

Thomas Ehrlich
*Provost, University of Pennsylvania*

S. El-Naggar
*World Bank Executive Director for North African and Persian Gulf countries*

Harry B. Ellis
*Senior Economics Correspondent, The Christian Science Monitor*

Yu Enguang
*Correspondent, New China News Agency (Xinhua)*

Richard D. Erb
*United States Executive Director, International Monetary Fund*

James R. Erwin
*Executive Vice-President, First National Bank in Dallas*

Clyde Farnsworth
*Economic Correspondent, The New York Times*

Henry H. Fowler
*Chairman, Goldman, Sachs International Corporation*
*Former Secretary of the Treasury*

James W. Fox
*Special Assistant, Economic Affairs, Department of State*

Lawrence A. Fox
*Vice-President for International Economic Affairs*
*National Association of Manufacturers*

Boyd France
*Diplomatic Correspondent, Business Week*

Isaiah Frank
*William L. Clayton Professor of International Economics*
*The Johns Hopkins University*

Edward R. Fried
*Senior Fellow, The Brookings Institution*

Robert W. Galvin
*Chairman of the Board, Motorola Inc.*

Jaime Garcia-Parra
*World Bank Executive Director for Brazil, Colombia, Dominican Republic,*
  *Ecuador, Haiti, and the Philippines*

W. H. Krome George
*Chairman of the Board and Chief Executive Officer*
*Aluminum Company of America*

Morris Goldman
*Economic Counsel, Office of Congressman Jerry Lewis*

Peter M. Gottsegen
*Managing Director, Salomon Brothers Inc.*

James P. Grant
*Executive Director, UNICEF*

Catherine Gwin
*Senior Associate, Carnegie Endowment for International Peace*

Fred L. Hartley
*Chairman and President, Union Oil Company of California*

J. Bryan Hehir
*Director, International Justice and Peace, U.S. Catholic Conference*

John M. Hennessy
*Managing Director, The First Boston Corporation*

Harriet Hentges
*Executive Director, League of Women Voters*

Ruth J. Hinerfeld
*President, League of Women Voters*

Hans C. Hittmair
*Deputy Treasurer and Director, Treasury Operations, The World Bank*

Dan Hoffgren
*Partner, Goldman, Sachs International Corporation*

John Holzman
*Financial Economist, Office of Development Finance*
*Department of State*

L. Oakley Johnson
*Director, International Economic Affairs*
*Chamber of Commerce of the United States*

Carola Kaps
*Economic Correspondent, Frankfurter Allgemeine Zeitung*

Samuel I. Katz
*Professor of International Economics*
*School of Foreign Service, Georgetown University*

Ismail Khelil
*World Bank Executive Director for Middle East countries*

Colby King
*Vice-President–Middle East and Africa, The Riggs National Bank*

J. Burke Knapp
*Former Senior Vice-President, The World Bank*

D. C. Korb
*Vice-President and Treasurer, Westinghouse Electric Corporation*

Joseph Kraft
*Syndicated Columnist, Los Angeles Times Syndicate*

Rolf Krueger
*Bureau Chief, German Press Agency*

Pedro-Pablo Kuczynski
*Minister of Energy and Mines, Government of Peru*

John J. LaFalce
*Member of U.S. House of Representatives*

Manfred Lahnstein
*State Secretary, Federal Chancellor's Office*
*Federal Republic of Germany*

Marc E. Leland
*Assistant Secretary for International Affairs*
*Department of the Treasury*

Seth Lipsky
*Associate Editor, Editorial Page, The Wall Street Journal*

Carol Long
*Washington Reports*

Anthony Ij. A. Looijen
*World Bank Executive Director for Cyprus, Israel, the Netherlands, Romania,*
*and Yugoslavia*

Gerald M. Lowrie
*Executive Director, Government Relations, American Bankers Association*

Hans Lundström
*World Bank Executive Director for Denmark, Finland, Iceland, Norway, and*
*Sweden*

Bruce K. MacLaury
*President, The Brookings Institution*

John L. Maddux
*Special Adviser, The World Bank*

Richard T. McCormack
*Department of State*

Matthew F. McHugh
*Member of U.S. House of Representatives*

Kay McKeough
*Acting Director, Office of Consumer and Producer Nations*
*Department of Energy*

Stanley A. McLeod
*World Bank Executive Director for Korea and South Pacific countries*

R. T. McNamar
*Deputy Secretary, Department of the Treasury*

Robert S. McNamara
*Former President, The World Bank*

Don May
*United Press International*

Constantine Michalopoulos
*Acting Deputy Director*
*U.S. International Development Cooperation Agency*
*Agency for International Development*

Arjay Miller
*Dean Emeritus, Graduate School of Business, Stanford University*

G. William Miller
*The Consultants International Group, Inc.*
*Former Secretary of the Treasury*

Theodore H. Moran
*Director, International Business Diplomacy, Georgetown University*

Joaquin Muns
*World Bank Executive Director for Spain and Latin American countries*

Reinhard Münzberg
*World Bank Executive Director for Germany*

Arnold Nachmanoff
*S. G. Warburg & Co., Ltd.*

Kimiaki Nakajima
*World Bank Alternate Executive Director for Japan*

Henry R. Nau
*Senior Staff Member, National Security Council*

William Neikirk
*Economics Correspondent, Chicago Tribune*

David D. Newsom
*Director, Administration and Programs*
*Institute for the Study of Diplomacy*
*School of Foreign Service, Georgetown University*

Jack Norman
*Reporter, The Wall Street Journal*

William F. O'Keefe
*Vice-President, Management and Budget, American Petroleum Institute*

James C. Orr
*Minority Counsel, Committee on Banking, Finance and Urban Affairs*
*U.S. House of Representatives*

Ferris S. Owen
*Vice-President, International Development*
*Cooperative League of the U.S.A.*

Henry D. Owen
*Senior Fellow, The Brookings Institution*

Wiegand C. Pabsch
*Economic Minister, Embassy of the Federal Republic of Germany*

John R. Petty
*President, Marine Midland Bank*

Gordon K. Pierson
*Director, Donor Coordination*
*U.S. International Development Cooperation Agency*
*Agency for International Development*

Art Pine
*International Economics Correspondent, The Wall Street Journal*

Ole L. Poulsen
*World Bank Alternate Executive Director for Denmark, Finland, Iceland,*
  *Norway, and Sweden*

Edwin Powers
*Staff Director, Subcommittee on Foreign Operations*
*Committee on Appropriations*
*U.S. House of Representatives*

Moeen A. Qureshi
*Senior Vice-President, Finance, The World Bank*

N. Ram
*Washington Correspondent, The Hindu (India)*

Myer Rashish
*Former Under Secretary for Economic Affairs*
*Department of State*

Himadri Narayan Ray
*World Bank Executive Director for Bangladesh, India, and Sri Lanka*

J. W. Redmond
*Partner, J. W. Redmond & Co.*

Harald W. Rehm
*Financial Counselor, Embassy of the Federal Republic of Germany*

Alfred Reifman
*Senior Specialist in International Economics*
*Congressional Research Service, Library of Congress*

Nicholas A. Rey
*Managing Director, Merrill Lynch White Weld Capital Markets Group*
*Merrill Lynch, Pierce, Fenner and Smith Inc.*

David P. Reynolds
*Chairman and Chief Executive Officer, Reynolds Metal Company*

Richard W. Richardson
*Director, Corporate Planning Department*
*International Finance Corporation*

Charles W. Robinson
*Chairman, Energy Transition Corporation*

David Rockefeller
*Chairman, International Advisory Committee*
*The Chase Manhattan Bank, N.A.*

Robert V. Roosa
*Partner, Brown Brothers Harriman & Company*

H. Chapman Rose
*Attorney, Jones, Day, Reavis and Pogue*

William V. Roth, Jr.
*Member of U.S. Senate*

Yves Rovani
*Director, Energy Department, The World Bank*

Hobart Rowen
*The Washington Post*

Robert W. Russell
*Staff Director, International Economic Policy Subcommittee*
*U.S. Senate*

J. Robert Schaetzel
*Writer and Consultant*

Edwin A. Schoenborn
*Senior Executive Vice-President, Irving Trust Company*

Enid C. B. Schoettle
*Program Officer in Charge, International Affairs Program*
*The Ford Foundation*

Charles Schotta
*Deputy Assistant Secretary, Commodities and Natural Resources*
*Department of the Treasury*

Hans Seidel
*State Secretary, Finance Ministry, Republic of Austria*

Roger D. Semerad
*Executive Vice-President, External Affairs, The Brookings Institution*

John W. Sewell
*President, Overseas Development Council*

Jill Shellow
*Quaker United Nations Office*

Roger Shields
*Vice-President, Chemical Bank of New York*

George P. Shultz
*President, Bechtel Group, Inc.*
*Former Secretary of the Treasury*

Horst–Alexander Siebert
*Economic Correspondent, Die Welt (West Germany)*

Leonard Silk
*The New York Times*

Lin Sloan
*Legislative Assistant for Foreign Relations*
*Office of Senator S. I. Hayakawa*

Gerard C. Smith
*President, The Consultants International Group, Inc.*

John W. Snyder
*Chairman, Harry S. Truman Scholarship Foundation*
*Former Secretary of the Treasury*

James B. Sommers
*Executive Vice-President, International Banking Group*
*North Carolina National Bank*

Alvaro Souviron
*Exploration Manager, Latin America, Anaconda Minerals Company*

Elmer B. Staats
*President, Board of Trustees, Harry S. Truman Scholarship Foundation*
*Former Comptroller General of the United States*

Sydney Stein, Jr.
*Limited Partner, Stein Roe and Farnham*

Ernest Stern
*Senior Vice-President, Operations, The World Bank*

Linda Stern
*Journal of Commerce*

Maurice F. Strong
*Chairman, International Energy Development Corporation*

Russy D. Sumariwalla
*Senior Fellow, United Way Institute*

Brooke Unger
*The Interdependent*

Vance Van Dine
*Managing Director, Morgan Stanley & Co., Inc.*

Frank Vibert
*Senior Adviser, The World Bank*

Frank R. Vogl
*Director, Information and Public Affairs, The World Bank*

Paul A. Volcker
*Chairman, Board of Governors of the Federal Reserve System*

Raymond J. Waldmann
*Assistant Secretary for International Economic Policy*
*International Trade Administration, Department of Commerce*

Charls E. Walker
*Chairman, Charls E. Walker Associates*
*Former Deputy Secretary of the Treasury*

Henry C. Wallich
*Member, Board of Governors of the Federal Reserve System*

Bill Wilson
*CBS News*

Guenter Winkelmann
*Alternate Executive Director, International Monetary Fund*

James D. Wolfensohn
*President, James D. Wolfensohn Inc.*

Montague Yudelman
*Director, Agriculture and Rural Development Department, The World Bank*

ISBN 0-8157-